ALSO BY MARTHA GRIMES

DOUBLE DOUBLE

A DUAL MEMOIR OF ALCOHOLISM

Martha Grimes and Ken Grimes

SCRIBNER

New York London Toronto Sydney New Delhi

Scribner
A Division of Simon & Schuster, Inc.
1230 Avenue of the Americas
New York, NY 10020

First Scribner hardcover edition June 2013

SCRIBNER and design are registered trademarks of The Gale Group, Inc.,
used under license by Simon & Schuster, Inc., the publisher of this work.

For information about special discounts for bulk purchases, please contact
Simon & Schuster Special Sales at 1-866-506-1949 or
business@simonandschuster.com.

The Simon & Schuster Speakers Bureau can bring authors to your
live event. For more information or to book an event, contact the
Simon & Schuster Speakers Bureau at 1-866-248-3049 or
visit our website at www.simonspeakers.com.

Manufactured in the United States of America

1 3 5 7 9 10 8 6 4 2

Library of Congress Cataloging-in-Publication Data is available.

ISBN 978-1-4767-2408-9
ISBN 978-1-4767-2412-6 (ebook)

To my old drinking buddies,
Leon and Harry,
And the place that came along and changed all that,
The Kolmac Clinic
Washington, D.C.

To my wife and sons. I do it all for you.
For all of the friends along the way who have helped me
become the person I am, especially Dayton, P.G., Fred P.,
Rich G., Eric, Cress Darwin, and Peter R.
Pass It On.

Double, double toil and trouble
Fire burn, and cauldron bubble.

—*Macbeth,* act 4, scene 1

FOREWORD

MY MOTHER AND I were sitting in a coffee shop talking, looking at the view of downtown Charlottesville, Virginia. This was ten years ago, and we had both been off alcohol for more than a decade. We were disagreeing about the best way to stay sober when my mother said, "I've been turning this over in my mind: I think we should write a book about alcoholism."

I sat back. "We?"

"Both of us. Two points of view. I think we should." It was the summer of 2002, and we were waiting for a real estate agent. My mother loves real estate agents; she's got a real hang-up about houses. She loves looking at them; she even loves buying them.

My wife and I had to take a more pragmatic approach. We were expecting a second child and we were, at last, going to leave New York City. After sixteen scintillating, maddening years, we wanted to trade in our Manhattan apartment for a suburban house. One possibility for relocating my business was Charlottesville, halfway between my wife's childhood home in Roanoke and my mother's place in Washington, D.C.

Sitting across from my mother with the coffee cooling, I was astonished by her suggestion that "we" should write a book. Easy for you to say, I wanted to tell her; no, I probably *did* tell her. "You've written books. I haven't. Who would want to read it? How would it work with two of us writing it? What would we say that would be of any interest to anyone? Who in hell would *care*?"

"A lot of people. A mother and son actually writing a book on addiction *together*? Parents of alcoholics would love it. They could see what I did wrong and what they did right. I mean, can you imagine *any* mom or dad emptying out a perfectly good fifth of Absolut vodka, then taking the empty bottle from Manhattan to Bucks County? I can see the head-shakers: 'I might not have been a perfect parent, but I certainly never did anything as weird as *that*.'"

I snickered. "But how could we write a book together? We don't agree about anything."

"That's the *point*. What child until he's eighty ever agrees with his parents? We'd have two different points of view, two stories coming from entirely different directions. I love it."

I didn't. Did we really want that kind of public exposure? Did we want to spill our guts and talk about every rotten thing that had happened to us because of alcohol abuse?

She shrugged. "I don't mind."

She would say that. Well, *I* minded.

Then I thought about it, about the differences between us. How she used an outpatient rehab clinic to get sober, and how I used (and still use) twelve-step meetings. When she was a teenager, she wasn't exposed to the same sorts of things I was. The teenagers she'd known didn't even drink. Hard to believe. She had no knowledge of drugs, promiscuity, Guns N' Roses, or actual guns walking the halls of her high school.

She'd missed all of that. I was literally marinated in it. I started drinking when I was thirteen, moved on to the harder stuff when I was fifteen, and crashed and burned when I was twenty-five. Twelve years sober and three-thousand-plus twelve-step meetings later, what was there to say?

"The word 'alcoholic,'" my mother said, "meant nothing to me. If anyone I knew ever mentioned our drinking, it would be in the context of drinking too much."

Why did it take ten years to write this book after our first discussion in that coffee shop?

Because we couldn't find another coffee shop?

The main reason is that I didn't think I could do it. Second, I completely underestimated the overwhelming amount of time it takes to raise a family. Third, I had a business to run; I thought such a book would present a certain image of me to my business associates, that I might very well lose clients as a result.

"You don't get it, Ken," she said. "They'd think you were cool, putting this out there. People respond to confessions with incredible sympathy. Don't you like reading about other people's bumbling weaknesses? I do."

"Does the world need yet one more recovery book?" I whined, sitting in our booth in the coffee shop.

"Yes," she said, eating her doughnut. "Ours."

I avoid reading recovery memoirs because my immersion in twelve-step meetings gives me constant exposure to what recovering alcoholics are working on, battling with, and laughing at right now. Also, I got sober before the recovery-book genre became popular, and it didn't occur to me to read other people's accounts when I had guys in the program who needed my help.

I still laugh out loud at the stories I hear in meetings. I just couldn't imagine a book having the same immediacy. Then one of my friends in recovery told me that he found books on recovery helpful as he was getting sober. That's my wish: that anyone reading this book will realize if I can do it, he or she certainly can.

I finally managed to make the time and find the confidence to write. Writing a book is a lot like stopping drinking. You do it one day. And wake up and do it the next day.

Easy for you to say, after being sober for twenty years! I can hear the reader protesting. Easy for you!

No, it actually isn't.

KG

PREFACE:
DOUBLE MACBETH

I<small>F THE WITCHES HAD</small> wanted to double Macbeth's troubles, their elaborate recipe of eye of newt and toe of frog should have included a pint of Guinness, a quart of vodka, a carton of Marlboro cigarettes, and a pound of marijuana. Or a very, very dry double martini.

I came of age in the "Just Say Yes" generation of the late 1970s and the early 1980s, between the end of the freewheeling 1960s—an era that my friends and I adored but which wasn't ours—and the dawning of Nancy Reagan's "Just Say No" decade of merciless greed and cocaine consumption.

How did I stop? With more than a little help from my friends. By going to meetings in recovery and finding people who are as crazy as I am. I've been sober for two decades and I'm still trying to change the saying "I may not be much, but I'm all I think about."

The literature of recovery says that letting go of the bondage of self is the only way to achieve that "priceless gift of serenity." Serenity from the screaming voices in my head telling me that I don't measure up, that I'm inferior, that the other guy is better-looking, that this woman has a better job, that everyone knows more than I do. Serenity is the absence of self, not of constantly thinking about me, and of sometimes actually thinking about others. Stopping drinking was the first step, because drinking is only a symptom of my disease. My fundamental problem is my lack of acceptance of the world as it is, as opposed to the way I demand it to be.

A person I really respect in recovery once said to me, "I don't know where I got this idea of having a pain-free life. My parents didn't tell me—not that I listened to anything they said anyway—nor did my friends, teachers, doctor, rabbi, or bosses. Somehow I grew up thinking that I shouldn't have to experience pain. If I felt any pain at all, anything that bothered me, I drank or smoked it away. I mean, that's the smart thing to do, right? The problem was that when I stopped drinking and drugging, I was a fourteen-year-old boy trapped in a twenty-five-year-old man's body because I never matured. I never learned how to deal with the normal disappointments, heartaches, and difficulties of life. The second the going got tough, I got going to the liquor store."

In the course of this book, you'll see that my mother's approach and my approach to sobriety are a little different. She hit the bottom and went to an outpatient rehabilitation center the day before Christmas 1990 and was a fan of that program for many years. Though she doesn't go to twelve-step meetings, she has come to grips with her alcoholism. We'd agree that *anything* that gets you to stop drinking and using is the right approach: organized religion, twelve-step meetings, living in a cabin in the woods, being an exercise fanatic. It doesn't matter. The one thing I kept telling myself as I was destroying my life with beer and pot was that they were all I had left. It's the supreme irony of addictions that what is killing you masquerades as the answer.

There is a theory in recovery that you stop maturing after you begin drinking excessively, and that was certainly my case. Getting sober at twenty-five was more than lucky; it was a power greater than I, working in my life.

Think getting sober is easier at twenty-five than forty-five?

As a friend of mine in recovery said, "It's not easy being young in recovery." Those of us in our twenties were a minority (albeit fast-growing). Plus, I hadn't done anything in my life to help define me, to give me an identity. No wife, no kids, no career. Nothing.

And the lies the disease tells you! I remember as a child watching the TV adaptation of *Sybil* with a (very young) Sally Field and wondering what it would be like to have a split personality. There's a reason why *Dr. Jekyll and Mr. Hyde* is popular: because alcoholism is beyond the yin-yang polarity of good and evil in all of us. From a nice teenage boy I turned into a monster, in a fury at the world for not being the way I wanted it to be. I was going to show them all, and if I couldn't show them, I was going to kill myself.

When I was new in recovery, I completely ignored the slogan "One Day at a Time" (which I've come to believe is the single most important message I've learned in my sobriety) because I could simply not imagine not drinking or getting high again.

Here are some of my early questions that proved to me I couldn't stop drinking:

"What about a business meeting when the client has a glass of wine? Won't I appear to be insulting him if I don't have one, too?"

I discovered later that the only people who care if I don't drink are those with drinking problems themselves. No one cares whether you drink as long as they get to drink themselves.

"What about dating? What if the girl I'm dating has a drink? Won't she think I'm a loser if I don't drink?"

Actually, no. If a girl is turned off by your nondrinking, you shouldn't be dating her. Before I got sober, I had to lie about the volume of my alcohol intake. I used my girlfriends as a control mechanism on my addiction, as monitors, and that's not a job anyone wants. After I got sober, I followed a very strict rule about dating. On the first date, after the normal chitchat and getting-to-know-you part, I would tell her at dinner I didn't drink and was sober X number of years. I was being fair to them, but more important, I wouldn't be tempted to keep it hidden and then want to drink that glass of red wine that was so large, you could wash a Buick in it.

"What, can't I have a drink on my wedding day?"

I didn't have a girlfriend. I was convinced the FBI was outside my door, and auditory hallucinations at work were beginning to be a distraction. I wasn't getting married anytime soon.

"How can I go to a football game without getting high?"

When I told my therapist that I had been stopped by the police in Washington Square Park for attempting to buy marijuana (I was let go without being charged, thank God for the non-Giuliani years in New York City), he asked why I had done something so stupid. "Because my regular guy was out, and I was going to go to the Giants–Eagles game, and I had to have some weed." When he asked why I had to get high to watch a football game, I had no answer except: "What's the point of going to a football game if you aren't stoned?"

I got married thirteen years ago and didn't have to drink. Now I can have a business meeting, go out to dinner with my wife, and go to a football game, and it simply doesn't occur to me to alter my state of being with chemicals.

Move over, Moses, because to those who really knew me, that's a real miracle.

MG
———

PREFACE:
DRUGSTORE

MARTINIS ARE MY DRUG of choice, straight up, on the rocks, vodka, gin, lemon peel, olive, onion, ten to one. Any martini drinker knows what I'm talking about. Liquid silver, that's how my old friend Harry described it.

Not, believe me, that I disdained other drinks—none of them, as I recall—being partial also to an old-fashioned, a daiquiri, a whiskey sour. But nothing could win me over like a dry martini, although one has to *acquire* that taste.

I was introduced to drugs when there was really only one hand to shake: alcohol's. Cocaine, heroin, marijuana, crystal meth: I was unacquainted with this happy quartet. I was school-age at a time when you could go to school without getting shot. That was a long time ago.

It makes no difference for the purposes of this book. Heroin and cocaine still rank as numbers 1 and 2 (despite the government's obsession with crystal meth), the baddest of the bad. Why split hairs? When it comes to addiction, they're all bad.

I'm going to avoid the big-ticket health issue, not because it isn't important but because it tends to obscure other issues. (When you set it against an X-ray of a cirrhotic liver, can you really convince someone that the drink on the bar is necessary?) You know, we all know, how dangerous addictions are to our health.

Nor will I talk about addiction as a disease. I don't know whether it is or isn't, but I don't care whether that martini shows I have a disease or an unquenchable thirst. I think I'll knock the "willpower" card off the table. It's way overplayed.

Most of life is engaged with filling a prescription. We fill up with whatever works at the moment: food, drink, smoking, shopping. A few hours at Target isn't quite as tasty as a few hours in Barneys New York, but it serves the same purpose. If you're starving, it doesn't matter who the chef is. And what works best is drugs. After the official drugs like marijuana and cocaine, alcohol (which, for some reason, gets separated from the others, for we speak of drugs *and* alcohol), we've got a long list: food (oh, what a drug lies there!), cigarettes, shopping, television, Internet, gambling, chewing gum, romantic love—anything that can fill the emptiness for a few minutes or hours or months, anything that comes from the *outside*, something that you don't have to work at. It allows you to escape, no questions asked, just go.

The whole world is our drugstore. We must be drawn out of ourselves by something.

Maybe that's why *Invasion of the Body Snatchers* keeps on being remade. The body snatchers are only after empty husks. Whatever was inside—call it mind, call it soul—is long gone, as with Gregor in *The Metamorphosis*.

In my hometown, there was a movie house, only one theater and only one screen and one balcony—no longer there, of course. When I was young, I would look around at the rows of people, the glow from the screen bathing their faces in ambient light. I was struck by how innocent the moviegoers looked, unguarded as children. They were drawn out of themselves; in a sense, they no longer inhabited themselves. This condition could change at any second: At the moment when the film fails to grip them, they become aware that they're in a theater watching a movie, which is failing to keep their attention, but suddenly, it can be captured again. Anything that erases us from time to time, that loosens our grip, relaxes us, and lets us breathe again. Anything except death, although at times I think that's where all of this is headed. We don't "breathe easier"; we're on life support. We've got all sorts of stuff skating into our systems to keep us alive, and we take this as good, even great, since we've left ourselves behind.

For the body snatchers.

We say we can't have a good time without a drink. Yet I remember years when I could have a sublimely good time without one. I was a little kid, or a bigger one, or even an adult. So why did I tell myself later on that I couldn't have any fun without a drink in my hand? A dinner party or any sort of gathering where we stand around and share small talk? No. You need to have a drink just to bear it.

A few years ago *USA Today* did a series of reports on dieting, a challenge they invited readers to take. One doctor or nutritionist—who did an incalculable service for all of us dieters—said that dieting is hard: "You might as well learn to play the violin."

That's how hard it is. Willpower be damned. Some *USA Today* readers probably thought the good doctor was brutally discouraging. I thought just the opposite: She told us what we were up against and why we failed time and again. When you fail in a diet you feel like a fool or a lout. Surely anybody should be able to turn down a doughnut. No willpower.

Stopping drinking is like this.

You might as well learn how to play the violin.

1

KG

—

Leaving Las Vegas

I had my last drink in Las Vegas, a sip of tepid Budweiser out of a waxed-paper cup at the Mirage casino on June 3, 1990.

I didn't plan on its being my last drink. I didn't really want to drink it. I was on a business trip and desperate to impress a pretty girl who said to me, "You're from New York, and you're not going to drink?" That's all it took for me to drink again, after holding back all weekend at the most important business conference in my nascent career. Some dreadful, reconstituted, none-of-the-original-members-except-one 1950s Motown soul group gamely pounded away as I drained half the cup of beer in one swallow. Just to show her I could party. I wasn't impressed with myself. Neither was the girl. Ever since then, I've hated Motown music.

I was part of a team responsible for putting on a book party to celebrate Donald Trump's new business tome, *Surviving at the Top,* which featured a self-satisfied Donald throwing an apple up in the

1

air. A follow-up to his surprise best seller *The Art of the Deal,* this book party was hosted by Steve Wynn at the Mirage, the first of the mega-casinos to swallow Las Vegas.

The trip began ominously on the flight from New York to Las Vegas. Turbulence over Utah was so bad that we were thrown from side to side, much to the alarm of the passengers, some of whom screamed in fear. I swapped stories with a producer from *Entertainment Tonight* and did my best to manage my fear like I always did: I read whatever I could get my hands on. According to a *Publishers Weekly* I clutched in my hand, Ken Kesey, one of my literary heroes and godfather of the counterculture, was driving the original Merry Prankster bus from his Oregon home to Las Vegas. He was promoting a new book, *The Further Inquiry,* a twenty-fifth anniversary of the exploits of my favorite band of LSD-fueled outlaws. My excitement over the Merry Pranksters and those pure, idealistic times that I was too young to have experienced made me overlook it as a shameless PR stunt. Strange, since I was a PR guy who was supposed to create shameless PR stunts.

Much to my delight, Ken Kesey and his pals had unearthed the bus from the backyard of his creamery in Oregon, cleaned it up, and were going to relive a little of the glory days. As my flight bumped through vicious turbulence, I ignored the hushed whispers and clenched fists of my neighbors. I closed my eyes to block it all out and remembered some of the best parts of *The Electric Kool-Aid Acid Test* by Tom Wolfe. It was one of my favorite books in high school, a real manifesto for the 1960s that I tried to copy by following the Grateful Dead, wearing tie-dyes bought in parking lots after concerts, playing Ultimate Frisbee, hitting on girls, and partying my ass off. At that point I had been to more than fifty Grateful Dead concerts, impressive by some measure but not many to dedicated "tour heads."

My cab dropped me off at the Mirage, where I was greeted by a fake volcano belching fire and Siegfried & Roy's white tigers pacing in their glass cages in the lobby.

The check-in lines were horrendous. When I finally made it to the counter, I was informed that they had no reservation for me. I would have to use my own credit card to guarantee my room. I indignantly tossed my credit card over and wondered if the tiny credit limit could handle the charge. I made my way upstairs to a Day-Glo claustrophobic room designed for one thing: to propel me into the casino. That began three days of nightmare conventioneering. Padding back and forth in our booth like one of the white tigers, I schmoozed with reporters and booksellers about the big books for the fall and the importance of our authors. The over-air-conditioned convention center and deep carpeting and hours and hours of talking without a drink gave me an almost hallucinatory, out-of-body sensation that spiked on the day of the big book party for Donald Trump.

After a four-hour stint in our booth, I had to get out to see Ken Kesey. I left the air-conditioned mausoleum and trudged across the impossibly large parking lot in the blinding heat toward the ramshackle bus. Tentatively, I stepped inside. The interior was much smaller than I anticipated, maybe because most of the seats had been removed and cots had been installed along the sides. Ken Kesey had transformed a long, narrow old school bus into one of the most iconic images of the era when the Pranksters waved their freak flag high during a journey across America.

It was all here: the intersection of parts of America that never would have dreamed of combining into one: a bus designed for innocent children to ride to school, driven by Jack Kerouac's famed lunatic, Neal Cassady, carrying Ken Kesey's Grateful Dead coterie to the furthest edges of LSD-fueled consciousness. I could feel it all inside the bus, and I desperately wanted to be a part of it.

I was disappointed that Kesey wasn't anywhere to be seen. A small group of modern-day hippies lounged in the bus. I looked around hopefully to see if they were ingesting anything of interest while thinking how much I missed going to Dead shows.

A wave of self-hatred hit me: I despised myself with my bourgeois-wannabe career, wearing my already out-of-fashion 1980s green Armani double-breasted suit with extra-wide lapels. I despaired of selling out to "the man." The same man, by the way, who was paying me to go on the business trip and allowing me the visit to the bus.

A Deadhead in a tie-dyed shirt and multicolored pants smiled and said, "Hey, man, how's it going?"

I immediately poured out my tale of woe to these chemically altered strangers, describing my meaningless life, my unsatisfying job, how everything after college seemed to be about money and career advancement.

I had been telling complete strangers my problems more and more, with increasing desperation. The previous month in New York, I had seen a local news profile of a man who sat on Madison Avenue and Fifty-second Street, in front of the Seagram Building, with a sign stating: FREE ADVICE. I tracked him down the next day and asked what I should do about my girlfriend breaking up with me. His answer was so unsatisfying that, as I walked away, I knew why his advice was free: "Don't worry, if she really likes you, she'll call you again."

I realized the Deadhead had been talking to me for a while: "Dude, it's okay, I mean, you're working this convention, and it might suck, but you're here in the bus with us now. That's good." How simple, how in the moment. It wasn't enough.

I mentioned I was working the party for Donald Trump later that evening. The lead hippie in the lethargic group snapped to attention. "Dude, you've got to get us in!"

"Okay," I said, confused as to how the conversation had taken this turn. I had a sneaking suspicion that letting a gang of drug-fueled hippies into The Donald's book party was a bad idea.

I looked around the bus at the half-dozen beaming faces. "Meet me outside the main convention room in the Mirage at six."

With an adrenal surge, I jumped off the bus and rushed back to the convention hall, where one of the senior executives at my company told me that a radio producer had stopped by to see me.

"Meet with that guy?" I retorted. "I don't have time for small fry like him!" I was half kidding, half not.

Fully anticipating a night of free food and girls to chat up, I became livid when my boss told me I was to be the doorman. I stood seething at the front door of one of the Mirage's cavernous ballrooms. Steve Wynn was the new king of the Strip, and Trump was on his meteoric rise, so this meeting of business titans was the hottest party at the convention.

I had to screen people and then tell them where to wait to have their picture taken with The Donald. I couldn't believe I had to work the event while my boss and the other executives were enjoying themselves.

I checked invitations and made wisecracks about Trump. Surveying the line of more than a hundred people waiting to have their photo taken with His Eminence, I cracked, "I wouldn't wait in line to meet this guy!" I noticed a sour-faced woman a few feet away with a pad and paper, scribbling something down, and it occurred to me that members of the press might be here. I blocked that from my mind and turned to see six Deadheads in full tie-dye regalia, with long hair and burning red eyes, charging up to me at the door.

"Dude! Can you still get us in?" one cried.

"Sure. In fact, you can cut in line right here."

I watched as members of the group attacked the piles of shrimp and ordered drinks from the bar while one held their place in the photo line. Books were stacked on a table near the door, and people waited patiently to meet Trump and Wynn, who stood in the middle of the room shaking hands and taking pictures. Through the dusky gloom of the ballroom, I could see the Deadheads closing in on Trump and Wynn. When they reached Wynn—who is legally blind and wears dark glasses—he seemed completely nonplussed by this assault on his person. Trump visibly gritted his teeth and looked around wildly for his PR people as the Heads gleefully snapped photo after photo and had their free books signed.

Just as quickly as they arrived, they disappeared.

"Ken, are you checking invitations in this line?"

I jumped and turned around to see the CEO of my company staring at me through her pink-tinted glasses.

"Of course," I said.

"There seem to be some people here who don't look like they belong." She paused. "So make sure you check the invites carefully."

"Absolutely," I answered, beginning to sweat despite the subzero air-conditioning.

Somehow, I returned to New York City in one piece and with a third-tier talent agent from Los Angeles stalking me by phone. We had met the night of the Trump party, and she fully expected me to take her up to my hotel room. I wasn't feeling it. I had her drive me around Vegas in her convertible and stop in one of the seedier sections of town so I could buy a cheap present for my assistant in New York. The whole weekend was weird, reminiscent of *Fear and Loathing in Las Vegas,* by another of my literary heros, Hunter S. Thompson. Without the bravado and drugs. Only the weirdness.

A week after Las Vegas, my boss called me into her office to confront me about my behavior, starting with bellowing at my colleagues in the booth that I didn't have time to meet a radio producer. Then she threw a newspaper on her desk. A story in a Connecticut newspaper about the book party reported "an employee of the publishing company said that he wouldn't stand in line to meet Donald Trump."

My boss looked me straight in the eye, her bushy hair standing up in the air. "So, Ken, did you say this? We're in big trouble if Trump or the editor of this book reads this paper, which is likely, since the editor lives in Connecticut and it's his local paper."

I lied so coolly and calmly, it reminded me later of lies I had told my mother for years about my drinking, friends, and general whereabouts. "No, that wasn't me. I don't know what that reporter was talking about."

My boss stared at me and said, "Okay. I believe you. But consider yourself under review. One more mistake and you'll be fired."

I left her office trembling and walked down the hall to my office. I stared out the window. If I lost this job, I lost everything. What would I do? Where would I go?

Back to Vegas?

2

Down the Drain

I t was somebody's birthday. A couple of friends, my agent, and her husband came over for a couple of drinks. For them, it was a couple; for Ken, it was none; for me, it was as many as I could put away before dinner.

I was the one who furnished the bottle of wine and made an inroad on the vodka and vermouth.

The next day I was leaving Manhattan for my house in Pennsylvania, where my friend Chris was deconstructing a 1950s bathroom for me. It occurred to me that it wasn't fair to Ken, who'd stopped drinking and joined A.A., to leave vodka in the apartment (that having been his favorite drink after beer), or wine, or vermouth, for that matter.

I poured the wine down the drain, then the vermouth. Bravely, I poured out nearly a fifth of Stoli. Then I was faced with the problem of the empty vodka bottle. The other two bottles had gone in the trash can. I was about to put the empty vodka bottle in but thought: Wait. If I do that, will Ken think I drank the whole thing? The empty wine and vermouth bottles didn't bother me, but an empty bottle of Stoli?

Here was my solution: I packed it in my suitcase.

An empty bottle to lug all the way to Pennsylvania. That made sense.

I got there; I unpacked. I took the empty bottle to the kitchen and was about to toss it in the trash when I thought, No, Chris might think I drank the whole thing. So I took it outside, up to the road, and deposited it in the trash that would be collected that afternoon.

Anyone whose relationship to alcohol isn't quite as obsessive would have done one of two things: left the bottle or taken it along. Why didn't I just take the full bottle to Pennsylvania? Chris was a big drinker. We could have swilled down the Stoli's together.

This, mind you, is what's called "alcoholic" or "addictive thinking." The whole approach to drinking is crazily mazelike. You turn left, you turn right, you go along, you go back.

Now, you—standing outside the maze, having heaps of laughter at the idiot in there who can't find his way out—please note: The idiot in there doesn't know it's a maze; he thinks this is the Capital Beltway or some other annoying, clogged-up, circular multilaner, but for all of that minor annoyance, it's the only way he can travel. This kind of thinking can also be called "denial." There are exits from the Beltway, clearly marked; there's an exit from the maze, unmarked. Much harder to negotiate.

So, you, standing outside at the exit, yell, "It's over here, stupid." But for her, where's here?

3

MG
___

Where's Here?
(Who's an Alcoholic?)

An alcoholic who is now in a twelve-step program, or who has otherwise stopped drinking, often cringes at the thought that others will notice and wonder why she's turning down that drink. The addict is sure everyone else at the party has a burning need to find out why she's refusing that drink. For the addict, it's all about her; it's all about me. Everyone will turn to look at me. Then, as if in a cartoon, these others will grow into huge, elongated shapes, taller and taller, and there's little me in the center.

If you take the more aggressive approach of telling your party acquaintance up front that you're an alcoholic, he'll be embarrassed to hear about it, unless he suspects that he's an alcoholic, too, and then he'll quickly disappear, or else he won't let you alone; he'll annoy you for the rest of the evening. He'll look at the drink in his hand as if he's never seen it before, as if it flew in out of nowhere, an alien with strange powers.

"Am I an alcoholic?"

Good question.

I'd say to the worrier, look at it this way for a moment: See that half-drunk martini sitting on the table over there? Whoever left it there isn't an alcoholic. Alcoholics might abandon their mates, their children, their jobs, or their cars along the road, but they're not about to leave a half-drunk drink sitting on a table.

Do you wonder whether you're an alcoholic? It's quite possible, if you're reading this book and can't find any other reason for it: You might be a parent worried about a child, or a child worried about a parent; you might be doing research on the subject; it might be too early to head to the cineplex around the corner. Reading this book will hardly brand a scarlet "A" on your forehead.

Here are a few standard questions a person might answer if he or she is wondering.

The first one, of course, is are you worried? The thought is that if you're worried, you have a problem; if you ask the question, you have a problem, because those who aren't alcoholics wouldn't think to ask the question (unless it occurred simply because you picked up this book).

Those who most willingly own up to drinking too much may not be alcoholics, since denial is the alcoholic's stock-in-trade, her first line of defense. (If one tries to eschew the notion of being an alcoholic by putting in its place "drinking problem," watch out.)

What about this—do you think about drinking when you're not doing it? A nonalcoholic wouldn't bother unless she were afraid that she wouldn't get to the liquor store in time to pick up the wine for the dinner party.

Another familiar question: Do you drink alone? Say yes and you're down a point or two in the magazine quiz. Drinking alone doesn't in itself peg you as an alcoholic. But if you say no, it probably tells you you're not.

I was told of a woman living alone who had exactly two highballs (if they still call them that) in the evening, sitting in her wing chair, reading a book. One could argue that anyone who is locked in to such behavior is probably an alcoholic. Well, maybe. It doesn't appear to be ruinous behavior, nor does her drinking increase over time. She stops with two drinks. Also, her tipple is the highball. Alcoholics don't mess around with that sort of dilution. Oh, an alcoholic might start out with a highball, but very swiftly, she's leaving out the water and down to the real business of drinking. (And it is a business, usually with set hours of operation, managed with meticulous care.)

I believe the craving for solitude is almost endemic to alcoholics. I've never known an alcoholic who didn't drink alone. Drinking and solitude appear as confederates in so many stage directions that there's probably a link.

A pragmatist could say you like to drink alone because you can drink more, and drink unsupervised by whoever is dying to say, "Haven't you had enough?," to which the answer is "No." The answer is always "No" as long as you've the wits to speak at all. Why don't people say what they mean? "You've had enough!" No one wants to take responsibility. Not the alcoholic but also not the wife, partner, child, or friend who asked that stupid question.

The alcoholic is irresponsible and undependable, it is said. At least I always turned up for my drink. You knew where to find me at five P.M.: in the kitchen or the living room with my ice-cold martini. I might have been the most dependable person in the state.

Right here. On the spot. Hard by the telephone in case anyone wanted to check up on me.

Solitude is the wild card in the drinker's deck. The love of it goes beyond avoidance of surveillance.

"Beyond all this the wish to be alone," wrote Philip Larkin. I've never understood people who can't bear to be alone. Frankly, I think they're worse off than alcoholics. People like that are usually nonstop talkers. Noise is the whole point. Noise, motion, lights, camera, action! Let me know I'm alive, for God's sake! Such people strike me as desperate.

"But you're a writer," someone might point out. "Solitude is necessary; to write, you've got to have it." I've written in restaurants, bookstores, Starbucks(es), airport lounges during flight delays, and so forth. Perhaps solitude is a state of mind you can carry around with you.

But solitude is necessary much of the time. Without it, I think I'd be made up of Post-its, sticking a bit of myself upon anybody or anything that happened along.

Here's my favorite anecdote about identifying an alcoholic. It might be apocryphal, but I think it did happen:

Dean Martin, Ronald Reagan, and William Holden decide to go for a drink. They walk into a bar. They have a drink. Then Deano and Bill agree: "Let's have another."

Ron says, "Why? We just had one."

Based on that evidence, you may not be able to argue that Dean and Bill were alcoholics, but you can bet the farm that Ronald Reagan was not.

"*Why?* We just had one."

That "why?" is a dead giveaway. "Why?" I cannot imagine myself asking this question in a million years. I cannot imagine myself asking the question even now, after all of this time, were I dumb enough to accept the first drink. "Why?" is not an alcoholic's question. "Where?" would be more like it.

If you were in that bar, who would you want to be sitting next to?

Me, I'd want to be wedged right between Deano and Bill. Cheers.

4

KG

—

An Introduction to Recovery

After I had lived in New York City for two years, my mother offered to help me move out of my tiny coffinlike apartment over an airshaft. My roommate and I shared about 150 square feet. He slept on the pullout couch in the living room/kitchen, while I crammed my miniature water bed into an eight-by-ten room.

My mother's mysteries had just started to appear on the *New York Times* best-seller list. She had put me through several private schools and college with her shrewd buying and selling of real estate. She volunteered to buy an apartment in Manhattan that she would own, on which I would pay the maintenance. It was a real gift for me on my eighteen-grand-a-year salary.

I found a real estate agent to guide me through Greenwich Village. The romance of Bob Dylan and the Beats and the renegade status of the Village was my poke in the eye to the typical post-college drunken frat boys who lived on the Upper East Side.

I trudged through the Village with my real estate agent, trying to find the best deal possible. It became clear to me that I wasn't the only one looking for parentally aided rebellion—everything was out of my price range. I slowly made my way north to Chelsea, a forgotten neighborhood that hadn't been gentrified.

Chelsea was the home of one of my favorite bars, Peter McManus, a hundred-year-old establishment on Nineteenth Street where you could sit and smoke and drink for hours without any irritating yuppies or dance music. I had spent many hours in the grand old Irish joint, with its delicious beer, a huge oak bar, massive mirrors, and surly bartenders. I needed to live in this neighborhood.

I found a very small one-bedroom apartment three blocks away and started making regular treks to Peter McManus. I was happy.

When I told my therapist why I'd moved to Chelsea, he paused and stared at me.

"Ken, don't you think it's strange that you picked a place to live because it was close to your favorite bar? Most people don't make that their number one priority when they look for an apartment."

I was speechless. There was no answer. No one had ever been this blunt.

After moving into that new apartment I was handed my first real assignment at the publishing company, a book on Adult Children of Alcoholics, a new concept. I heavily identified with the different stories, and reading it released a torrent of blame toward my parents, which conveniently excused me from taking responsibility for my own actions.

But it stirred something in me about my own drinking. In a moment of honesty, I went to the Employee Assistance Program and told the counselor a fraction of the truth of how much I drank. She insisted that I call a therapist who specialized in alcohol and drug addiction.

I called the therapist, and for the next year and a half, I fought with him about going to twelve-step meetings and why I had to quit drinking and smoking pot. He worked with me to see that my obsessions weren't natural. I refused his entreaties to attend twelve-step meetings and denied that my drinking wasn't normal, even for a twentysomething Manhattanite. He patiently put up with me as I rambled on about my girlfriends—or lack thereof—my parents' drinking, my problems at work, and my general unhappiness.

I finally capitulated and reluctantly took the phone number of a guy my age in recovery. I went home to my apartment, picked up the telephone, and called. I had an hour-long conversation with a guy who was a year younger than I was, seemed pretty cool, and assured me that you could have fun without getting hammered.

I was astounded. I quizzed him on how you could go to a Martin Scorsese movie not loaded, a party and not get fucked up, meet a girl without a beer in your hand?

He answered all those questions and uttered the last words any alky wants to hear, "So, why don't you go to a meeting with me tomorrow night at eight?"

I mumbled a yes and dropped the phone on the receiver.

The next day, I thought about the meeting constantly during work and took the subway uptown with dread to the appointed address. I approached the church and saw a dozen people in the entryway talking, smiling, joking. I tried to avoid them and scooted downstairs, where the guy I had spoken with somehow seemed to know who I was—was it the wild eyes? The sweaty brow?

17

I remember nothing from my first meeting—most people don't—but I do recall recoiling in horror when the people beside me reached out to hold my hand and chant a prayer. Wait a second, what's with the praying? Isn't this supposed to be nonreligious? I'm an *atheist*.

That was it. I hated this program. I ran to a pay phone on the corner and called my best (actually, my only) friend and blurted out that I had just been to a twelve-step meeting.

He responded neutrally. "Well, I hope that doesn't mean we can't have a beer every now and then."

As I progressed in early recovery, I slowly came to understand that the questions for all recovering alcoholics are not how we arrived at our sorry state and who's to blame but why we continue to create a hard-knock life for ourselves while sober. What does the twelve-step literature mean when it describes a life that is "happy, joyous and free"? Is that something I really want? My mind says yes, but the rest of me, that emotional core inside me, isn't so sure and would prefer to burrow into a cocoon of negativity.

A recovery friend of mine once said, "I went to the doctor to have my blood checked—"

Another friend interrupted, "And it came back negative!"

It came back negative, because I am negative, even as I stare at the positive accomplishments in my life. Simply staying sober for over two decades is a singular achievement.

Still, I seethe at the petty injustices and my unmet needs as proof of the world's ultimate injustice. I never got enough, never had enough, never will get enough. Not only is my middle age the winter of my discontent, it's often my every waking moment of discontent. What banishes the discontent? Meditation. Running. Going to the theater. Absorbing nature and its beauty is a kind of relief. But the thing that sits inside me, waiting, lurking, I can't let it off the leash because it's part of me.

Many years after I got sober, I was at a cocktail party with my fiancée, and an acquaintance accosted me to discuss his problem with alcohol. He asked, "Ken, you seem to have done it. How? What did you do? What can I do?"

Not having shared with him that I was in recovery, I paused and thought, What the hell, I'll tell him the truth. "What did I do? Let's see, I went to a couple thousand recovery meetings, went to individual therapy for ten years and group therapy for seven years, and I'm still taking boxing lessons for anger management."

He gave me a startled look, said nothing, and disappeared back into the party to get another drink.

5

"I'll Be Back on Monday"

I imagine the Kolmac Clinic was familiar with the "I'll be back on Monday" dodge.

People who walk through the doors of a rehab clinic, especially outpatient, probably do it under duress or in desperation. They've just come off a weeklong bender or gotten arrested or lost their job, their house, their life, and figure they've got to fix this. Now.

Except that after a sobering half hour or so of talking to the doctor or counselor or therapist, "now" has a funny way of dragging its feet into "later." And "later" never comes around at all. So the potential candidate for clean and sober does not come back on the next Monday or any Monday until he goes on another hair-raising overdose that doesn't kill him and resolves into another "now" arrival at the clinic. This time maybe he stays, but probably he doesn't.

The look that Dr. Kolodner gave me as I told him I was going out of town for the weekend but would be back on Monday made me wonder how many people returned. I'd have bet they were few.

Me, I'm reliable. He wasn't impressed. All Dr. Kolodner seemed to know was that once out the door was one time too many.

"I'll be back," I said, and rose.

"It would be better to come to the group tonight."

"Well, I've already made plans to go out of town."

"Can't the trip be postponed?"

"No. I didn't realize you'd want me to start going to sessions right away."

"Yes, I do."

He unnerved me a little, but I was impressed by his intensity: The man really, really did not want me to walk out that door. I felt almost ashamed for doing it. I'd known him for fifteen minutes, and I already felt I was letting him down. His look was almost poignant in its distrust, not of me but of drugged promises.

I knew I'd be back. He didn't. The thing was, I hadn't been shoved through the door by someone else—by a relative or an intervention or a cop or a court order. I'd come on my own. Great, I could hear him thinking. She who comes on her own can leave on her own.

I was back on Monday.

The Kolmac program required my presence for three hours a day (or evening) of group counseling/therapy, five days a week. This lasted for eight weeks, but over that period, the number of days per week gradually decreased. This amount of time did not strike me as unreasonable. There were other choices, A.A. being one.

Another was an inpatient clinic that would have had me there around the clock for four weeks.

Before I decided on Kolmac, I arranged an interview with an inpatient clinic, the usual twenty-eight-day stay (which I've always thought absurdly short). This was a posh place near Leesburg, Virginia. It was lovely; it looked like an antebellum mansion, a beautiful house in a green world of lush grass and live-oak trees.

The young woman who showed me around the elegant rooms informed me of the schedule the patients were supposed to keep: regular group meetings every day, individual meetings with therapist or psychiatrist, and time-filling projects of a recreational nature such as art or pottery.

Dread. All I could think of was my mother's nursing home and sitting with her in the "art" exercise group. She would paint already formed pitchers and vases in pastel colors. It was close to a paint-by-numbers exercise. My mother had been, among many things, an accomplished watercolorist. What she was doing now was so far beneath her abilities, it made me want to weep.

I said to the young woman, "No, that sort of arty exercise I don't want to do. I can spend my time writing. I'm a writer." I seemed to have forgotten I was entering a world of nonnegotiation, where "don't want to" wasn't in the playbook.

She looked displeased. Then she astounded me by saying they preferred that patients not bring to this experience anything they'd been doing before.

"Like shooting up? Yes, I can understand that."

Brief smile. No, anything. Do nothing that you did before to pass the time. To do what you did before coming here might hinder recovery. What you did before got you into the mess you're now in. She didn't say it, but that is the commonly held belief.

That ended that interview.

As I drove off, I thought hers was a very poorly thought-out response to the situation. She must have thought so, too, because in a few days, I got a call from her saying it would be all right if I wanted to write in my "spare time."

I thanked her but said I had already signed on to another facility, an outpatient clinic.

I hated the round robins of the first hour of Kolmac clinic meetings. I asked the counselor who led our group why information gathered in this go-round-the-circle way (the kindergarten circle, I didn't say) couldn't as easily, and to better purpose, be gathered if we spoke spontaneously.

Because we have to make sure we check in on everyone. Presumably, not everyone would speak if not called upon. Fair enough. But I didn't believe people in the group wouldn't speak unless spoken to.

That first hour was, if not an actual time-waster, a time-killer. I was a teacher for too long not to know what time-killing was. I'd done it often enough in class, going through some bit of writing or exercise I thought basically meaningless because I had to get through the hour. We were committed to the clinic for two hours at a shot, and the hours had to be spent.

The second hour, in which we spoke spontaneously, was the one in which disappointments, unhappy home life, traumatic incidents were revealed. In that second hour, silence sometimes fell. I always liked the silences. All of us sitting there, sharing it. I felt the experience was more real than a lot of the talking. One doesn't fake a silence.

Eventually, it would be broken by one of us talking about something that had happened, or by a person saying he couldn't stand the silence. I liked that, too; it was honest. What didn't sound honest were the banalities, the bromides, the ill-thought-out descriptions of our time since we'd last appeared here. In a way, we were forced to come up with platitudes, the most popular of which seemed to be: "Well, I had a busy week." Did this, did that. Yes, you did. So did I. So did everybody. But what aren't we saying?

Funny, I never heard any of us say, "I had a shiftless week." Or a bone-idle week. Or a didn't-do-one-damned-thing week.

What I kept forgetting, or possibly never understood in the first place, was that the business at hand was to keep people from drinking. The aim was not to understand why what we did contributed to our need to drink—although understanding wasn't discouraged; it was welcomed. The point was that understanding oneself was not the way to stop drinking, though it might make it seem less robotic. This point cannot be overestimated: The purpose of both the clinic and A.A. was to keep us from drinking.

I think many of the group members realized the purpose of these rituals was to keep them from drinking; if there were rules they didn't especially like, they were perfectly equipped to put up with them. I seem to think any group gathering not held in church or Starbucks is group psychotherapy. That could be because I'd been to more psychiatrists than Woody Allen.

I love analyzing things—things, people, events, myself. I expect that's why I couldn't sit back and be calm and let it all wash over me. There were others in the circle as analytical as I was but were smarter about the purpose of this circle.

One day a couple of people in the circle were glowering at me as I banged on at yet another kettle of Kolmac fishiness. Finally, one woman said, "I don't know why you stay. You obviously don't like this. You'd be happier someplace else."

I'd be happier? Don't you mean you'd be happier? Are you that unaware and yet not dead? Nonetheless, I took umbrage at the general murmur of assent. Actually, I was shocked that I was being fired from my own group—forgetting again that this was not group therapy and I could be a danger to their sobriety, or so they might have felt.

Sobriety is a coldhearted game, make no mistake about that.

I'm not sure anyone even wanted to understand why he or she drank; they just wanted to stay stopped. I don't see how that's possible, ultimately, unless you keep up the relationship with either a clinic or some other group, mainly A.A. That I didn't think I could stay stopped was why I went to the clinic for so long, every week for around two years. (That and my horror of leaving anything—a place, a person, a house, a landscape.) Kolmac knew the danger, which was why they kept urging people to go to A.A. meetings.

So, off I went from the clinic. I don't believe I had a plan. If I did, it was like that of everyone else who quit the clinic: not to return to the old drinking style.

It was some time—weeks? a couple of months?—before I drank anything at all. I started with a glass of wine. Then two. It was a while before I was back on vodka.

After a year or two and a nudge from my son, it was back to Kolmac.

In my defense, I'll say this: Dr. George Kolodner and Jim McMahon (the cofounders of Kolmac) were wrong in thinking that my complaints about the group were an excuse to leave. This time I was in another group and I liked it. These people didn't think I was a danger to them; they didn't think I was trying to stiff them somehow; they didn't think I was an albatross around their necks.

This time I stayed.

Alcoholics Anonymous's prescription for success is ninety meetings in ninety days. If you can do that, you have a fighting chance at long-term sobriety.

I would imagine that anyone who attended a meeting every day for three months would be well on his way. Ninety meetings would make attending a habit, and anyone willing to go to ninety meetings in ninety days isn't just dropping by to see if A.A. suits him.

I wasn't that person. I really tried, though. All told, I went to perhaps twenty or twenty-five meetings. I went to meetings in Georgetown, Santa Fe, Seattle, Jackson, London, Martha's Vineyard, and even Florence, Italy. Georgetown and Santa Fe, for the most part, since I lived in both places. The one in Jackson was about as far removed from the sunny slopes of Jackson Hole as one could get. The meeting took place in a church basement; it was a congenial gathering of guys in boots and Stetsons with tobacco-stained fingers and a couple of women in fringed skirts. Yes, that's what they wore in Jackson.

Every drinker knows the pleasant anticipation of a party: the crowded smoky room, the drink in hand, the one or two you had ahead of time to oil up. Everyone standing around with glasses and small things to eat and cigarettes.

The meetings had this odd schema of a party—you know, the way a party breaks up into little groups. One group hung around the coffee urn (which, in happier times, would have been the drinks table); another group stood near the door smoking; another was off in a corner, munching on cookies.

A meeting was as uncomfortable for me as a party because I could never seem to attach myself to one group or another until I'd had a few drinks. I think that most alcoholics feel this way. Alcohol is the grease or the lubricant that eases us into social situations. Deprived of it, I would stand around like a stick. A drink was a kind of compass that would point me in the right direction in a social gathering. Without it—to my alcoholic way of thinking—there was no True North.

To me, an A.A. meeting made for a very dingy, poor, bleak party, with its coffee and cookies, since A.A. does not have money to waste on parties. It felt a little like a run-down country club to which I hadn't been offered membership. So set down extreme self-consciousness as one reason for not liking the general atmosphere before the meetings.

I disliked the self-fulfilling prophecy of the twelve-step program. I did not object to the twelve steps themselves (well, not most of them), but I did object to the sleight of hand that said if you go back to drinking, it's because you didn't follow the twelve steps. That strikes me as saying you're drinking because you're drinking.

It wasn't that I disdained meetings, and I certainly didn't disdain the people who attended them. I had the same problem with A.A. that I had with the clinic—trying to analyze everything. Except that in meetings, people let you go ahead and say any dumb thing you wanted to, including whatever negative things you had to throw out about not liking A.A. It might be the only place where one experiences total acceptance.

That was during the meetings. Before and after, I felt invisible. There was the circle at the end, the Lord's Prayer (which struck me as leaning a little too far away from A.A.'s espoused secularity). It didn't end every meeting; many ended with the A.A. prayer: "Give us the strength to change what we can," et cetera. But I do recall joining hands in a circle—indeed, a double circle because there were so many present. I kept trying to wedge my way in but was always a shade too late, and another hand was grasped, not mine. I didn't make the cut. This affected me deeply. I blamed myself for not trying hard enough, but how hard do you have to try just to get in the circle?

It's possible that I'm what A.A. calls a "dry drunk." (I dislike the designation because I believe jargon and slogans have limited usefulness. But A.A. likes them, possibly for that very reason. "Keep It Simple," so you don't start overcorrecting the ambivalence by hauling in all of the reasons for not drinking, which undoubtedly would lead you to haul in all the reasons in favor of drinking. The slogan is equivalent to "Just Say No.")

A dry drunk is one who doesn't have a drink but is still holding on to the glass. You're not waiting for the host to come over and fill it, but you are aloft, or afloat, or in drinker's limbo, somewhere other than with your sober feet on the ground. This state of mind has you clinging to the shreds of your old drinking existence; you're the undead.

The trouble is, you've got this empty glass, but you're not seeking something to fill it instead of vodka. A.A. (and the clinic) wants your life refashioned, since it was the old way of living that got you into the mess to begin with. I've never exactly understood the nature of the refashioned life, that is, beyond the obvious: One doesn't hang out in bars with former drinking buddies. Indeed, I think one injunction mightily severe: You also get rid of the drinking buddies. Throw out the baby with the bathtub full of gin. I doubt that affected many of us, as friends are generally there to do more than bend an elbow on a bar.

I find the concept of the rearranged life is fuzzy. What are the old "habits"—besides drinking—that one is supposed to jettison? If you're a tennis player, are you supposed to stop? If you play the violin, are you supposed to lay down your bow? The only concrete examples of what you're not supposed to do are 1) drinking; and 2) hanging out with your drinking friends. I've noted this before. I've also noted that it's blindingly obvious. The only thing I've ever heard argued is the hanging out with friends. But I have never been given any other concrete examples of what one is not supposed to do.

As with the cryptic slogans, I think the nebulous advice to stop doing what you were doing before is fairly useless. At best, rearranging one's life has limited value.

My life is largely a writing one. Almost exclusively a writing one. Before, it might have been a writing and drinking one. Now that it's no longer a drinking one, that leaves the writing one. I don't see how I can stop doing that, even if I thought I should. And I don't.

FIRST CONVERSATION:
GENERATIONS

MG: It seems to me, whenever I see teenagers and their parents represented in a film or read it in a book or magazine article, the teenager is always obnoxious in his attempts to get out from under the watchful eye of the parents. You weren't. You were usually charming, and that's one of the reasons I didn't really notice a lot that was going on.

KG: Once I started drinking beer and smoking pot behind your back, if you weren't the enemy, you were certainly the jail warden. And like any convict, I had to get over on you. I was no longer a little kid, but I wasn't an adult; I was an adolescent on an alcohol- and drug-fueled tear, and nothing was going to get in my way, including you. The traditional things to look for in teenage drug or alcohol abuse are grades slipping, petty lawbreaking, a belligerent attitude, and a different set of friends. I grew my hair long, and that changed my appearance, but you didn't seem to mind. A lot of people had long hair in the 1970s; it was the style for men. The paramount concern for me when I started "partying" was getting away with it, and I knew the best way to get away with it was to fake everything in front of you and my teachers—all authority figures.

MG: Me being the primary authority figure, since I had to play the role of both mother and father after your father's disappearing act.

KG: You bet. As you said, I must have had a natural degree of charm, and without even realizing it, I doubled down on that aspect of my personality. I know I consciously tried to make people laugh so they'd like me. Also, I was never one of those teenagers who wanted to do shit like boost things from the 7-Eleven or get in fights or steal from people's cars. I just wanted to get high and party with my friends and chase girls. My question for you is: Did you have any idea what was going on, or were you in denial and trying to fool yourself? Remember that time when you picked me up from school and asked me why my eyes were so red and I said it was because of my allergies? Did you know my eyes were red from smoking too much pot? Did you believe that half-assed lie? I was stoned out of my gourd.

MG: I had no idea at all. There are two things. One is that I really didn't know about marijuana smoking back then. I knew nothing about drugs, and I would have had no idea it made your eyes red. The second thing is you were lightning quick with your answers. If you had stammered or stuttered and seemed nervous or guilty, I would have been suspicious. You were always in there with the answers, every single time. I still remember standing in the kitchen when you were in high school, and I was telling you a whole series of things I wanted you to do. You just stood there nodding, dutiful.

I'll bet when you were stoned, you stood and looked me right in the eye, like a victim of locked-in syndrome. You had a peculiar ability to muffle this stuff. I knew there was something going on in the woods after you got caught by the teachers in ninth grade for smoking pot. It was a failure on my part that I didn't do more about that.

KG: You had no idea? You didn't smell the marijuana on my clothes or on my breath? Because I was high constantly from the second half of ninth grade through my junior year of high school.

MG: No. That's what I said: I wouldn't have known what I was smelling.

KG: On the other side, I knew many kids who've told me about their drug use and drinking, and they would always tell me about their parents, many of whom were drunks. They couldn't invite their friends over; the parents were passed out on the couch. That wasn't the case with you, because you drank but never showed the effects. I can think of only a handful of times that I thought you might be drunk, which is amazing, considering your martinis had at least three shots of vodka in them, and you drank at least two a night, along with some wine. The effects were more joking. And when you got together with your brother or some of your college-teacher friends, the witticisms had more of an edge. You were probably reenacting what you went through with Mrs. D., your mother's business partner, who was so jovial during the first few drinks but then could become quite cutting in her comments.

MG: Yes and no. There was a big difference: Mrs. D. got completely paranoid and consequently unapproachable and inexplicable. I didn't, nor did my brother, nor my friends, ever go that far. Mrs. D. was so much fun in the beginning. But she could become completely irrational.

KG: Alcoholics are usually very undependable. But your drinking never impaired your driving, you never missed a day of work, dinner was always on the table, so I never really understood what was going on when you lost your temper over what I thought were pretty small issues, or suddenly became furious and got in an argument. It was because of the booze, but I didn't know that. I remember one time in college going to a friend's home; he told me in advance how funny his dad was and how much he liked to drink. I met him, and the first thing he did was pull out a bottle of vodka. But what got me was he pulled out a fifth of vodka, and I just assumed that all parents who drank kept half-gallon jugs, like you did, with the built-in handle. His bottle seemed hilariously small in comparison. I knew there was excitement around drinking, I loved making your martinis, I was a bartender at one of your parties when I was twelve.

MG: God.

KG: And it was confusing because there must have been times when you were hungover or not feeling well, or the alcohol was making your depression worse. I couldn't figure out what was going wrong. I never connected the second or third martini with your getting angry and frustrated.

MG: Isn't that one of the troubles right there, that people don't or can't make a connection between alcohol and quixotic behavior? I had no idea about alcoholism when I was twenty-five, couldn't even imagine it. I would imagine some people would say to me that I didn't know what you were doing because I denied it, and I suppose that's a possibility, but on the other hand, there was such a gap between the 1950s and the 1970s, between your generation and mine. I mean, when I grew up, the only drug I knew about was cigarettes, and the first time I smoked a cigarette, I was a senior in high school—and my mother bought me my first carton of cigarettes when I graduated.

There were no drugs for me and my friends. They just weren't there. I remained stupid about drugs except alcohol for most of my life and most of yours. I found your pipe in the basement when you were a senior in high school, and I didn't say anything about it. I don't know why; I just really didn't know what it was for. Of course, when you were suspended in the ninth grade for smoking pot, I took you to a drug counselor at a halfway house— that was the level of sophistication about teenage drug use in 1979—and he told me you didn't have a problem.

KG: Yeah, I really got off the hook then, because I hadn't graduated to harder drugs yet, and my pot smoking wasn't completely out of control at that point. I hadn't earned the nickname of "Spent Ken" (as in burned out from smoking too much pot) yet; that happened in tenth grade. If I had told my counselor the truth at age sixteen, he would have enrolled me in that halfway house imme- diately. But at that point, the truth was in my favor, and the counselor didn't see occasional pot smoking as a real problem.

MG: Yes, so there's another example. Combine that with the headmaster at your high school, who was so blasé when I confronted him about the pot smoking in the woods. He said, "What do you expect me to do, put a fence around the woods?" I was astonished at his thinking he was unable to do anything. These were the people in charge, and they refused to take your behavior seriously, to take action.

KG: And you sent me back to my childhood psychiatrist when I was fourteen. I had seen him when I was six and off and on through elementary school. But he wasn't interested in my pot smoking; he was interested in how I felt. So I went to my weekly sessions stoned. He did tell me once that if I kept on getting high, we weren't going to get anywhere, but he really didn't see drinking and getting high as a problem unto itself.

MG: No, but give him some credit. You yourself claim that addiction is a symptom (while at the same time claiming it's a disease—work that out, will you?); clearly, a psychiatrist believes that, and wants to get at the way you feel, since the way you feel is the problem, not what you're taking to douse the feelings. My own psychiatrist simply didn't believe I was an alcoholic, which was what I wanted to hear. I argued with him about it, I said I do this, I drink this many martinis, and he just let it go. My editor couldn't believe it when I said I was an alcoholic, either.

KG: Because he was an alcoholic!

MG: Maybe, but that's not the point. A number of my friends could have been alcoholic or had a "drinking problem." The trouble is that people think that it's so clear-cut; they think that an alcoholic is just someone who gets drunk and falls down, acts like a drunk. But that's often not the case. It wasn't with me for decades.

Psychiatrists want to figure out what the underlying problem is, and their record for getting people sober is very poor. I don't think you can manage your drinking without eventually going right back to where you were, drinking uncontrollably every day. Consequently, it's both difficult and simple—what is lying behind wanting to pick up that glass of booze is a massive complex of reasons, all tangled up together. You don't understand what you're up against. You have no idea.

KG: That's for sure.

MG: Also, I feel that you had too many advantages. For instance, when it came to responsibility for financial commitments, you knew nothing. You never really understood the cost of your college education, you just thought I should pay it for it, and I say that makes you at least somewhat spoiled. You've said that you think you were selfish and self-centered but not spoiled? What's the difference?

KG: Well, to me, a person can be an extremely hard worker and put on a good front, but he's still essentially thinking about himself with little regard for other people's feelings. "Spoiled" is someone who expects to receive a lot with very little effort, doesn't have to work hard for what he receives, has been overpraised for his abilities, and thinks he should win just by showing up.

MG: What about your behavior from high school graduation through college and beyond? My feeling is that you should have gone to the University of Maryland, because I had to pay for most of it, and that was all I could afford.

KG: That's completely different. Look, people in twelve-step programs see it like this: Because things were so bad for me at the University of Iowa, it was crucial to my getting sober. It had to be terrible enough for me to even consider stopping drinking. I collapsed three years after graduating from college and got sober. Your point is valid, the University of Maryland is what you could afford, it was in-state, Iowa was out of state and much more expensive and I practically died there, but it sped up the process, and I got sober when I was twenty-five instead of thirty-five or forty-five.

MG: There's something wrong with that argument. What I'm talking about when it comes to spoiled is overindulgent parents. When I think of it now, letting you go to college at a place I couldn't afford was wrong for that reason and that reason alone. I was indulging your desire to get away when what I should have said was too bad, you have to go to UM. After you got to Iowa, your behavior was terrible. You spent too much money, didn't take difficult enough classes, didn't get good enough grades.

KG: Yeah, and that's where I went off the deep end.

MG: The Western Union scam for five hundred dollars was outlandish and a real example of the streak in your nature of putting stuff over on me.

KG: I tried to put things over on you, all right. And you're talking about a generational difference. With my generation and my sons', I'm wise to the game, so there's no being caught off guard—

MG: Oh, really? Well, good luck with *that*!

KG: No, no. They could try, but my kids would have a very hard time outfoxing me. I wrote the book on that. Children not really understanding their parents drinking, parents not really understanding what their children are doing, whether it's how much they're drinking or if they're sneaking drugs or not. That will never change, the back and forth, it's so hard to gauge the amount and the effect.

MG: I guess I just assumed you would do what I did—wait until college before you started seriously drinking.

KG: Yes, your drinking started slowly and then escalated when you were in your twenties, right? Mine began in earnest when I was fourteen. And you didn't have the drugs to complicate everything. Some teenagers supposedly can "drink safely," whatever that means. But how much is that? One beer? Four beers? Are "boys going to be boys" and get up to hijinks with drinking, and is that just a normal rite of passage? Some parents tolerate a degree of drinking under their watch so as to take the forbidden-fruit aspect of it away, the allure of it. Some parents have zero tolerance, some don't pay attention, no one knows how much is too much until it's obvious, like a drunken car wreck or getting busted. With you, I was consuming far too much alcohol and drugs, and I was able to hide it, and when I went to college, I didn't have to hide anything anymore.

That's where all of a sudden I went off the cliff, because I didn't have to fake it anymore. I tried to use my girlfriends as a way of controlling it, using them as a kind of governor to throttle back on my consumption. That would work temporarily, then we would break up and I would step on the gas. I used my first job out of college as a control mechanism; I would just party on the weekends, but that made me miserable.

Then I crashed.

6

MG

Stopping

The number of drinks I had every evening is a bit of a blur (how surprising!), but I'd guess four or five martinis. And one has to consider who's making the martinis. One of mine might equal two of any bartender's.

I did this drinking before dinner, always, never after. I never wanted to drink afterward. And I always ate dinner. One might ask, If you only drank during cocktail hour, what's the problem?

How long is your cocktail hour?

I stopped drinking between Christmas and New Year's—to be more exact, on New Year's Eve. But wait a minute: I stopped before, *before,* the magic hour of midnight, New Year's Eve. I stopped despite a dinner date at a swank restaurant. Why didn't I allow myself that one last wonderful binge, like any sane alcoholic would do?

Because I told myself it would be better not to turn those last wee hours into some grand drama of martyrdom and sacrifice. In other words, don't lend the occasion too much significance. Better not to allow alcohol center stage; better not to clothe it in such gorgeous raiment that I would let it precede me to my table. No, let it walk around in rags, let it be refused admittance to the dining room. Sorry, Stoli, not this time. Goodbye, Grey Goose, go fly in somebody else's airspace. Henceforth, I will walk in on the arm of sobriety. I will refuse to attach a lot of importance to drinking.

As if I could. The notion that any alcoholic could attach too much importance to drinking only shows how naive I was.

Naive and arrogant. I didn't wait until New Year's Day to stop, because I insisted upon having a handle on drinking before I even knew what a handle was. I had no idea what I was up against. I was, admittedly, extremely proud of myself. And you should be proud of yourself, considering what you're placing on the table; just not as proud of yourself as I was five minutes after I'd stopped. Wait at least half a day before you're proud of yourself.

Arrogance got me through both New Year's Eve and the week that followed. I remember walking past a bar in Georgetown, looking in, thinking, Oh, you poor guys, look at you, finding the only happiness you can in booze. How pathetic.

But then the next week, after I'd been kicked out of Arrogance, Inc., I was back at that bar with my nose pressed up against the glass, mouthing, Please, sir, another helping of gin, please.

There's something simple about drinking: You can stop only by stopping. "How do I—?", for an alcoholic, is the wrong question, because there is no "how."

"You're saying that I'm supposed to stop something so entrenched in my psyche I can't tell where the drink on the bar ends and the rest of me begins?"

That's right.

"—the one thing that makes my entire life supportable?"

Yes.

"—that'll get me through those boring parties?" (Or lively ones.)

Right.

"—and without something to put in its place?"

Because there is nothing to put in its place. Nothing substitutes for your drug of choice, for the substance of an addiction. What would you put in its place? Food? There is nothing that the bartender can put on the bar, or the waiter on the table; nothing cooked up by Jamie Oliver or Julia Child or all the chefs at the Bellagio that would make up for the loss of a dry martini.

You stop by stopping.

Intelligence has nothing to do with it. Understanding has nothing to do with it, which is the reason psychiatry has never had much luck with alcoholic patients. Alcoholics Anonymous might be considered a "how to stop." But even there, it isn't "how." Although the twelve steps might look like a directive, I don't think they are; the steps are simply supportive (which is not to diminish their importance). The twelve-step program is not a way of toning down your drinking; it is not a method that tells you how many drinks to have and in what proportion and at what time and with what ingredients. That's because the twelve-step program is not a methodology but an ideology: The intent is to change your life. It is not telling you how best to drink but how best to live.

You might compare it with dieting. There is every manner of recipe advising you how to take the pounds off: what to eat and how much of it, all the substitutions you can make for high-fat food, how much of this to consume and how much of that. Dieting is a methodology, with hundreds of new variations coming out every year. Its instructions, its recipes, are precise.

There's no recipe for ending an addiction. Unless you consider this one: Here is a glass. It has vodka in it. Do not pick it up.

In the Kolmac Clinic, there was one rule: If you decided to quit treatment, you would come for one last session and tell the rest of us "Goodbye-and-why-I'm-leaving." This was never a popular assignment for those who were quitting.

The reason the quitters gave was always the same: "Since I've been here, I've learned that I can control my drinking," or some variation on that theme. "I believe I can take one or two drinks now without slipping back into my old ways."

No, you can't.

Such reasoning always astonished me, since it was precisely that inability that landed the person in the clinic in the first place.

Ah, yes, I can take one drink . . .

The blessed first drink that goes down like fire stolen from the gods (and you can bet they're looking forward to payback), the deliverance, the relief from the sharp-edged day, from party anxiety, from boredom outside and in-, from the empty night.

It's at least as good as holy water. You relax and become not exactly another person but a better version of this one. Who would not want to hold on to that feeling? You'd have to be mad not to want to. So here comes the tray with the fresh drinks, and you take one, which is the second one, the one you told yourself you weren't going to have. A little later, the third one steals in on little glass feet.

You can fool around with recipes. You can set limits for yourself. Perhaps you'll become a weekend drinker. You can try it, but it probably won't work, or not for long. Indeed, it only prolongs the misery. If you start weekend drinking, you'll still have five days to get through, and you'll spend them waiting for the weekend.

The weekend becomes the only time you feel alive. It's Friday. Let's live! So you spring the cork or pop the top or twist the cap. This will work, you think. And for a while it does. For one or two weekends, or a month or two, or even six months.

But listen: What of the wasting away of the rest of the week? Of those blighted five days? The five days you can hardly wait to end, to get to the weekend.

There are any number of variations on this theme: "I only drink at parties," "I only drink after dinner," "I only drink during the Sunday game," "I only drink to unwind after work, especially on Fridays, with the other working stiffs."

The problem was that I couldn't stop. I decided not to drink on any given night. I tried to do this any number of times. Sometimes it worked; more often it didn't. A few times I told myself I wouldn't drink for several days. I was back to drinking within forty-eight hours. I wouldn't have lasted a week in the weekend-drinking scheme. The question was not whether I was an alcoholic—I was pretty sure of that—no, the question was, did I want to be?

Why stop? My health was in no immediate danger; drinking wasn't affecting my writing output. So why stop? Because I couldn't. And if I couldn't, something other than my own dimwittedness was in complete control of me. Thus, my inability to stop began to outweigh the pleasure of drinking.

Which is not to say that drinking was ever an unvarnished pleasure. The first drink was the comforting balm that would have lulled Odysseus if he'd hung around in the land of the lotus-eaters; he knew he would never get back to Ithaca.

The next couple of drinks had me spiraling upward. Every problem solvable, everyone approachable, every book writable. That would be half the evening. After that, the other half, a downward spiral. You've heard it a hundred times: Alcohol is ultimately a depressant. But there was something positive even about the depression: insight. Insights in this swamplike thinking would be awfully insightful. Feelings would be honest, searing.

Or at least that's the way it felt.

Even if all of the insight and honesty were real, I'd wake up in the morning and be the same old me with the same old problems. All of that expansive thinking was as airy and fluttery as a hummingbird's wing. Not that I couldn't remember it, but it meant nothing.

I wasn't the smartest girl in the room after all.

How do you stop? There are several routes.

You can join A.A.; you can go to a clinic; you can see a psychiatrist; you can align yourself with the group that believes you can control drinking through "management."

The first two work; the second two usually don't.

It's simple why the first two work: They tell you to stop drinking. Period. Stop, and *then* we'll talk about it.

Stop.

You can choose to see a psychiatrist for reasons other than drinking. I had my coat pockets full of psychiatrists, the last one for over fifteen years. Alcoholism was only one of the topics, and it ran out rather quickly, since he didn't think I was an alcoholic.

(No one did except me. And the director of my clinic.) There's the hope that you might uncover the reasons why you drink. But it won't help much even if you do.

People seem to think if you've identified a problem, you've licked it. You've seen the light; you've had an "Aha!" moment. That might happen, but you haven't licked it. After all, why should the problem be solved simply because you've identified it? You can understand why you do something, but that doesn't take away your need to do it. It's the need you're hung up on.

You don't stop drinking by analyzing;

You don't stop drinking by understanding why you do it;

You don't stop by thinking about it or "reasonably" deciding to cut back;

You stop by stopping.

This is bad news. It's hard to think you can't somehow nibble around the edges of the problem, maybe suck on the lemon twist or the olive; that maybe you can cut this quitting into workable parts.

There are no workable parts. You might think the twelve steps are workable parts. But they're meant to strip you of your ego, your old self; they don't strip the glass from your hand. The only requirement for membership in A.A. is the desire to stop drinking, not the stopping itself. If the glass falls to the floor, that's a by-product.

There is an advantage in accepting this: It lets you off the hook for searching out some plan or trick to get you to stop, that will convince you to stop, that will talk you into stopping. There is no trick.

That old ace in the hole is, simply, stop.

7

MG

Cauldron, Bubble

I never knew the strength of alcohol's embrace until, midway through my childhood, Mrs. D. came along. My mother had inherited a summer hotel from her father, and Mrs. D. helped her run it.

Although my family had produced all kinds of sots, neither my mother nor my father was a drinker. But along came the business partner, Mrs. D. (which is what we called her), and boy, could she drink. And she did it in style: always dressed for cocktail hour, always primped and powdered. Every evening at five, I could hear her approach across the cavernous dining room, announced by the rattle of ice cubes in a pitcher and glasses on a tray.

When I was in my early twenties, that came to be a sound as welcome as the theme of *The Twilight Zone*—which was where we wound up, back in the office behind the front desk. We always sat there in case a potential guest should require lodging.

The back office was a narrow little room that housed a rolltop desk and swivel chair, where Mrs. D. sat; a black safe; and the bentwood chair I used. If a third party should join us, he or she sat on the windowsill. My mother would sometimes stop by and share a cigarette and some laughs, but not for long, since my mother actually worked.

There was another side to Mrs. D.: her inexplicable anger, usually directed at me. We'd pass each other walking through the dining room, and the air would crackle. One reason I hung out back there was to short-circuit the fury Mrs. D. felt much of the time, something that might erupt at any time except within the confines of the back office during cocktail hour. Get us in the back office with our old pals, Jim Beam and Gordon, and we could slip right back into being old pals. Even as an adult, I felt that frisson of fear when I would pass her on the steps or in the dining room.

Knowing this about alcoholism, knowing anything about it, would have saved me a lot of adolescent misery. I knew nothing because the word "alcoholic" wasn't invoked to explain why someone was slobbering drunk; that was just "drinking too much." One of the hotel guests falling down the stairs? "He drinks too much, *tch tch.*" Another guest yelling in the dining room? "She really should cut back on the cocktail hour." Laughter. The concept of alcoholism wasn't discussed. I have an idea that the word was as toxic as "cancer"—a word spoken in hushed tones, if at all. Alcoholism wasn't on the table. Thus did we avoid staring it in the face; thus did we circumvent the awful mystery of addiction.

Mrs. D. did not have to be in the depressive stage of her drinking to go into one of her frozen rages; they could happen at any time. Alcoholic feelings persist even when one isn't drinking. We say, "Thank God she's sober today." But she isn't; an alcoholic is never sober in the sense that feelings disappear when the actual drinking stops. Mrs. D. was always in the grip of alcohol, whether or not she had a drink in her hand. And the rage was usually directed at me for some infraction of her vague and shifting rules. Sometimes I knew what I'd done, but more often, nothing was clear, I had to bet on what had caused her anger. I usually lost. She would not speak; she would not say what was wrong beyond the occasional "You know what," if I asked her what I did. So it was like trying to second-guess a blackjack dealer.

Since Mrs. D. was furnishing a good deal of money to keep the hotel above water, my mother wanted to avoid an uproar, a sudden packing of bags and leave-taking (a thing always threatened and once acted upon, so the threats were not idle). My mother's response to me over Mrs. D.'s massive unreason was "Just apologize." "Apologize for what? I don't know what I've done!" "It doesn't matter. Apologize." She was speaking to an extremely unapologetic person. I had to stand up for myself; nobody was watching my back. I tried to sit with my chair against the wall in case Mrs. D. walked into the room.

Yet she would do things for me that seemed a complete reversal. She bought her clothes at a pricey boutique (before that became such a nifty little word). One day she left a large box in my room. Boxes of high-end merchandise always have a luster and satiny feel that the cheap boxes don't. From this one I pulled a truly beautiful dress that went to the floor. It was much too old for me, which was part of its charm. It was a blue-gray linen, very plain, unadorned except for some white beadwork around the square neck. I think its elegance came from its simplicity. It would be in style today. The more I think of that dress, the more I wish I had it now.

(Where do these things go? We wind up with a storeroom's worth of things we've accumulated over the years that we don't want, yet the things we prized somehow got away from us.)

Still, there was that anger, a boiling cauldron, taking very little inducement to overflow. Very little to anyone else, enormous to her, because in her state of drunkenness, things were incalculable. Eventually, the reason for the anger would come out, and it would be a strange brew she had stirred up, eye of newt, toe of frog, bits and pieces mixed from her distorted notion of what had happened or was happening. She might have begun with something resembling reality and then reinvented it by cooking it too long in the cauldron, by thinking and thinking about it. We can all turn a neutral and passive act into one bristling with implications and then go to work on the implications until we have worked out a whole little world.

With her, the entire machinery of alcoholism was at work. I recall once when she was in bed, sick but not too sick to enjoy cocktail hour (alcoholics are rarely that sick). My brother and his wife brought her a calla lily in a pot as a get-well present. She pointed a finger at them, accusing them of mocking her husband's death thirty years before, when lilies had flowered at the altar and been laid on his casket. (In the several years she had been at the hotel, I had never heard her mention her husband.) It was a charge so far-fetched, only a paranoid would love it.

The overthinking of an incident, an imagined slight, perhaps, or an old conversation or chance comment invests it with a peculiar power. The bed, the pointing finger, the white lily made a scene out of a Poe short story; it was certainly Poe-esque in its paranoia. The "It" of alcoholism—call it the wolf, the devil, or one of Macbeth's witches rising up within—you project on whoever is offered. In this case, it was my brother. He was the devil come to mock her dead husband.

And yet there were the back-office cocktail hours where Mrs. D. and I were thick as thieves. There was something larcenous about it, stealing time from the hotel business. Why should a couple of hooligans be hanging around drinking in the office when my mother was breaking her back in the kitchen?

It was more fun, wasn't it? We had more laughs in the back office than out in the kitchen, watching the intricate construction of a meringue crust filled with a cloud's worth of lemon chiffon, or listening to the sizzle of hot oil in a pan into which quarters of chicken dusted in pistachio were dropped and prodded with the tines of a long fork.

In the back office, the edibles were tiny pretzels and cheese crackers. The sliver of lemon peel, the half-capful of vermouth, the Gordon's or Smirnoff as cold as an iceberg. Jokes, quips, laughs. Drinks.

Occasionally, Mrs. D.'s daughter, M.J., would join us and take the windowsill seat (as there wasn't room for another chair). M.J. was taller, older, and blonder; I was smarter. I think one problem was that Mrs. D. liked me more perhaps than she liked her own daughter (it was my misfortune not to recognize it). We looked enough alike that people in town started calling me M.J., although I had lived there most of my life and M.J. had come on the scene only four or five years earlier. My life felt taken over.

In the cocktail hour, grudges were forgotten; injustices justi-
fied; wounds, if not healed, cauterized by Jack Daniel's or Gordon's gin.

Sometimes we would repair to the "family table" in the dining
room, where my mother would join us without her apron and
with a cup of coffee. These were rare occasions. Usually, I stayed
behind the desk while Mrs. D. had dinner. Someone had to man
the desk.

Afterward, I would go to the kitchen to eat. I *never* missed
meals. I always had dinner, no matter how late. No, I wouldn't
have missed it for the world or for a drink. The food was too good.

My mother was a divine cook.

"Anyone who can read can cook," she would say as she was
combing *The Joy of Cooking* for a recipe that she would add to or
subtract from to suit her own taste (this immediately cast doubt
on her theory).

What her cooking alchemy took must be akin to something
the writer does with words, adding and subtracting intuitively. A
word feels right or doesn't. You might use a recipe of Julia Child's,
but it will not turn out like Julia Child's, because you are not Julia
Child. It might be as good; it might be better. Something is lost in
translation. There is some intuitive understanding of the way food
works.

My mother made the best Roquefort-cheese salad dressing in
the world. The requirements were simple: Roquefort (or other
blue cheese) and olive oil. A simple recipe, a monumental amount
of patience. I would watch her add the oil to the cheese drop by

drop in an electric mixer. Too much oil and the whole thing would curdle. The key ingredient was patience. Drop by drop. I tried to make it and never succeeded. I was too impatient.

Head chef, chef de cuisine, sous chef, chef de parti: She was all of them. And not only at the hotel; we acquired a large brick pillared house in town that we turned into an inn. She did the cooking there, too. Many nights would have her driving back and forth.

On top of all of this cooking, she would make slipcovers for the armchairs in the lobby of the hotel, upholster furniture, make me an evening gown.

When I think of this now, I'm staggered by the excess of talent she demonstrated. Was this woman ever appreciated? By her father, the one with the intractable wife? By this stepmother, who spent her days on a wicker chaise longue, invalided out of performing any duty? (My mother was doing a lot of the cooking even when she was a teenager.) By me? No. Nor by my brother. Did Mrs. D. appreciate her? I don't see how she could have, given her volatile nature.

The one time I recall the word being used was when my mother said, "If I had the time, I'd be an alcoholic." Most alcoholics would chortle at this, knowing that one can always find the time for a drink. Always. I thought this amusing in its naïveté. Now I'm not so sure there wasn't a lot of truth in what she said: Work, especially such all-encompassing work, can keep you sober.

I think sometimes alcoholics feel they've vaulted onto some other plane, clearing the high bar of time and circumstance. We're extremely self-absorbed. We're all wrapped up in a sort of alcohol aesthetic that sees the simple picture as impossibly naive. Alcoholics like to say "Keep It Simple," and this is all too true of the simple instruction: "Stop." Despite the bumper-sticker slogans that arise from keeping it simple, alcoholism, or the defeat of it, becomes a truly complex business.

Couldn't the circumstances that my mother found herself in have kept her safe from addiction? One striking difference between her and Mrs. D. was that one worked and one didn't. Or at least for Mrs. D., work never interfered with drinking. Cocktail party? Out the door.

I'm not talking about the kind of work that leaves one hand free (like writing) to pick up a glass but the kind of work my mother did, ten hours a day or more, seven days a week. I can still see her, walking down the long second-floor hallway, white apron wound about her. At six A.M., heading for the kitchen to make the Parker House rolls for a dinner party that evening.

Time and circumstance. Maybe she really didn't have time to be an alcoholic.

I wonder if my mother felt excluded from the back-office brawls and how she explained the exclusion to herself. Or if her answer was to imagine the dinner party—the pastry still cooking in the kitchen, the poached pears, the crème anglaise. The mint sauce that she needed for the lamb. I wonder if work was as close to salvation as she could get.

Why didn't I learn to be a good cook instead of a good drunk?

Why didn't I spend my postprandial hours in the kitchen instead of the back office?

I recall once when I was in my twenties and in England, writing my mother a letter of apology for things I had done that made her unhappy. It was a long letter full of self-pity and sorrow. She never mentioned the letter when I came back. Finally, I asked her what she thought about it. She said she'd never received it.

Sometime later, she asked me to search out something from

her dresser drawers. In looking, I found the letter down in a corner of the drawer, buried beneath blouses and slips.

Another instance of this failure to acknowledge emotions occurred after an interview for the *Washington Post Magazine* years ago. The interviewer was with me for some hours, up until the entrance of my brother and his second wife. We were going out to dinner. We hung out for a while with the journalist, had a drink. In the published piece, the writer said that I changed the minute my brother walked in. I became another person.

This surprised me, although I was conscious of sometimes retreating around my brother, who had, to say the least, an entertainer's personality. What surprised me more was that I heard nothing from him. No call, no question, like "What in hell does this mean?" No response. The question buried, like my mother's letter, in a bottom drawer.

Burying emotion exacts terrible consequences. Thus are psychiatrists called into play. A psychiatrist can do a lot, but only as much as the patient can stand. And there it stops.

Buried emotions, especially anger. You know how brutal the anger you're conscious of can be. Imagine the brutality of the anger you've buried. Rage can be terrifying, for it seems endless, limitless. Probably it is. There is no bottom to the cauldron. It doesn't appear to have what T. S. Eliot called an objective correlative: an object that can be identified as a reason for an emotion. (Eliot's prime example is Hamlet; nothing in the play adequately explains his inability to kill Claudius.)

I think this was the problem with Mrs. D. and me. That I didn't know what the reason was for her anger became almost a metaphor. Because even when I thought I knew, I didn't know. Neither did she.

She poured alcohol on it. I did, too, to a lesser degree. That got the anger down to embers, but it still burned, and after not too long, the flames shot up again.

Because nobody knew what caused it. Except that we caused it, a kind of double arson.

Double, double toil and trouble,
Fire burn, and cauldron bubble.

I wonder if there are things that, if acknowledged, would sink us faster than any fifth of gin. I wonder if there are ways of behaving that we simply cannot manage, like a tearful goodbye, or even a tearful hello.

My father died when I was five. I remember my mother telling me about his death and adding, "Don't cry." I might have looked at that injunction throughout my life as bearing more weight than it merited. "Don't cry" is so often a knee-jerk response to a situation, doing little more than marking the other person's responses. It's a breathing space while you think of something that might be more comforting. "Now, don't cry." "Be good." "Be quiet." Phrases that are the mere ghosts of meaning.

Given half a chance, put a foot wrong, and we're all capable of going down. We know we're standing at the edge—and what does a good stiff drink do? Pulls us back just in time.

Hello. Goodbye.

Don't cry.

If I think on all of this too long, I will be overcome by lack of purpose, failure, or nostalgia.

Nostalgia, someone once said, is the death of hope.

I guess I won't drink to that.

8

Hawaii Five-0

To paraphrase Joseph Heller's *Catch-22,* some alcoholics are born, some alcoholics are made, and some have alcoholism thrust upon them. I earned an A in all three categories. My experiences when I was eleven and twelve living in Hawaii would be in the "made" category. Trying to escape from my life through books no longer worked. Having to fend off the bullies at a new school, followed by the loneliness of being by myself six hours a day in the college library at the University of Hawaii where my mother taught English, was the harbinger of what I would embrace in high school.

During the bicentennial summer of 1976, we rented our gray shingle home in middle-class suburban Washington, D.C., and temporarily moved into a rental in the Ilikai hotel in Oahu. Situated in downtown Waikiki, it was famous as one of the locations for the filming of *Hawaii Five-O*. I even appeared as an extra in one episode, striding confidently behind Jack Lord as he hurried by the swimming pool on the way to meet Danno.

Summer was over too soon. I had to stop spending hours alone at the pool and the beach where I gazed at the girls. In Washington, D.C., I was lucky to attend a small, relatively inexpensive private school based on the philosophies of German philosopher Rudolf Steiner. I was used to small classes. No bad behavior was tolerated, the teachers were completely devoted to their students, and the students were expected to obey their teachers.

Here in the middle of a verdant paradise, my new junior high school campus was old and dirty. The palm trees drooped as if tired from the years of bearing the weight of children. The grounds were worn, the grass a dull green, and the school buildings like Quonset huts from World War II.

I hated going to the school's bathroom. Located in a small building separate from the main school building, it was small and smelly. Several of the older Hawaiian boys seemed to spend most of their time in there. When I went in on the first day of school, they grinned at me and said, "Hey, brah, want to buy a joint? Only a quarter."

I didn't know what they were talking about, but the fear coursed through me as I washed my hands. "No, thanks."

"C'mon, you don't want to get high wit' us?"

They all laughed as I dried my hands and fled. My radar to the outside world signaled "Don't hurt me." Teenagers can sense weakness and how to exploit it.

The next day on my way to class, I was startled to find one of the local Hawaiian kids falling in beside me. "So, what's your name?" he said in a friendly tone.

"Ken."

"Ken, I don't have no lunch money. C'n you give me some?"

I put my hand in my pocket and felt the quarters. "No," I said cautiously. I could feel the shame flooding my body, because he knew, and I knew, that I couldn't stop him. I was too scared to fight.

"Well, brah, see, that's gonna be a problem, because if you don't give it to me, I'm gonna have to take it." He smiled.

Walking quickly, I reached into my pocket and gave him four quarters.

"Yah, thanks, Ken. I really 'preciate it. I won't bother you again." We both knew that this was just the beginning. He was going to take my lunch money every day.

The idea of going to a teacher was laughable. The teachers were terrible. In many of the classes, they didn't bother to give lessons. They just handed out workbooks with questions to answer. Math class was the most painful, because although I was good at math, I didn't retain it well over the summer and needed a little help at the beginning of the year to remember the basics. This math teacher started giving out problems, then testing us during the first week of class. I couldn't remember how to solve the problems. I started crying quietly, the tears burning. I rubbed my eyes so no one could see, and tried to figure out the different equations. I was ashamed that I couldn't provide the answers.

By the third week of school, my mother complained to the principal about the bully constantly stealing my lunch money. The principal was a nice man but ineffective. "We asked the other boy, and he said he didn't do anything. So there's nothing we can do. It's his word against your son's."

A hopeless situation.

We moved to Pearl City, near Pearl Harbor, to live in a two-bedroom in a high-rise condo building with a swimming pool. Instead of school, it was studying alone at the University of Hawaii's library while my mother taught.

Here, in the most beautiful place in the world, my mother sat in her room and typed, and typed, and typed. The result was her first Richard Jury mystery. A novel set and steeped in rainy England, written in balmy, fragrant Hawaii.

I was into science fiction then: I read all of Ray Bradbury, Arthur C. Clarke, and Isaac Asimov. The main branch library in the old part of downtown Honolulu is famous for its beauty. I spent many hours there, marveling at the quiet, at the statuesque banyan trees by the entrance, the palm trees rising above the chairs in the open courtyard, the sweet-smelling air with hints of flowers and the sea. We didn't have a car when we lived there. I rode the bus everywhere around the island. I read *Catch-22* on those buses, and Frank Herbert's *Dune*.

But I could read only so much. It was here that the painful parts of adolescence took over. The desperate longing I experienced in looking at yet barely being able to speak to some of the most beautiful girls in the world—all of them older and with nothing to say to a twelve-year-old—drove me crazy. I began to have nightmares like the ones I'd had when I was little of people trying to kill me, and several times I experienced a druglike disembodiment in our elevator, a sensation that I was looking down on myself from above.

My loneliness became more acute. Like any twelve-year-old, I wanted to distance myself from my mother, to make friends. I was the new guy, the stranger, and younger than most of the kids there. My first month at the condo complex, I tried to befriend some teenagers.

One day they realized I was afraid to swim in the deep end of the pool. "What's a matta with you, boy?" they said to me in their mock-Hawaiian accents as I was splashing in the shallow end. They were all sons of navy men and were intimidating. They teased me relentlessly when they saw me mooning over a beautiful thirteen-year-old girl.

"Don't tell us you can't swim!"

"Well, no," I admitted. "I don't know how to swim."

"Don't know how? Ah, c'mon, we'll teach ya," one said, and they all smiled at one another.

I walked from the shallow end of the pool to the deep end, and one of them shoved me in. I plunged into the water, my feet not touching the bottom, and came gasping to the surface. I dog-paddled to the wall and looked up at the ring of smiling teenage boys.

"See, you know how to swim!"

It was in Oahu, riding the buses by myself, that I developed a neurosis I have to this day—a terrible fear of getting lost. I dream about it constantly, being on a bus or a train, not being in control and not knowing where I'm going, the surroundings familiar but somehow backward, like a tape playing in reverse. When I'm driving and I lose my way, panic takes over; my chest tightens, anxiety ripples through my body, and I speed up to outrace my fear.

I asked the bus drivers in Oahu repeatedly, "Is this my stop? This one? You won't forget to tell me?" Though the bus drivers patiently answered my questions, my fear remained.

Not long after I was thrown in the deep end of the swimming pool, I went to the surfing beach Waimea Bay. With stands of coral and booming surf, Waimea is famed for its tubelike waves. The beach was largely deserted on a weekday. I didn't know about the wicked undertow that drowns even accomplished swimmers.

I went into the ocean, fascinated with the tall, graceful waves, how they thundered against the large coral ledge to my left. I kept dog-paddling out to the point where I could see down the vast cylinder tube that a wave would create. It seemed as if I could see fifty feet down the tube before the wave curled down and crashed into the surf.

Suddenly, I was caught in the undertow. I flailed and "swam" as hard as I could but got no closer to shore. I kept at it for what felt like hours but couldn't have been longer than ten minutes. Finally, I crawled to shore and flopped down, terrified and exhausted. A kindly man asked if I was okay, and I gasped out some kind of reply. When I went home, I didn't tell my mother.

As the year progressed, I studied in the college campus library every day. I've spent so much time in so many libraries that whenever I visit one, it brings back a flood of childhood memories. Books were my friends. When I'm in libraries or bookstores now, looking at the shelves of books, hundreds of books, thousands of books, I feel reassured, content.

That wasn't my year of living dangerously, but it set the stage for what was to come. These experiences in Hawaii added to the "made" category. Soon to come would be high school, where I'd meet new friends who would push me into "thrust upon me."

9

KG
——

Crossing the Rubicon

So, you don't get high?" said one of my classmates in amazement. It was my first week of ninth grade in an experimental high school program that fused academics with camping and hiking trips.

"No, but I've gotten drunk before. Twice," I said proudly, hoping that would get me over.

The group of kids looked at me and then at one another. "Ha, we'll call you the boozer. You're so uncool." They moved on, with their blue-jean jackets and long hair, smirking and making jokes.

It was starting all over again, and this time I knew I couldn't take it. Not after a year of reading by myself in a college library in Hawaii. Not after a year at the Catholic junior high school where I was humiliated every day. I knew I couldn't survive being an object of ridicule again. I knew that drugs were bad, period. I didn't want to do them just to fit in, and I didn't, declining my classmates' offers for almost a month.

I wrote in my diary on October 14, 1978, two weeks before I turned fourteen, that I had decided to "cross the Rubicon" and smoke marijuana for the first time (I was a Roman history buff with a flair for the dramatic). The first time, I didn't feel much of a sensation, just tired and a little out of it. My friends studied me for signs of change, hoping they had "given me my wings," as junkies say about turning someone on for the first time.

The third time, I felt the full effect. After smoking some blond hash, I flopped around in a semi-psychosis on the grandstand in the auditorium, and I felt better than I ever had before. My new "friends" liked to get high; I loved it. The sensation of being free, of being silly, of colors and sounds and the light all reflecting back to me, was sheer bliss. It was a sensation that I would chase for the next eleven years, even as it became harder and harder to recapture. I upped the quantity and variety of drugs, but no matter how much more I consumed, they worked less and less.

I was quickly accepted by the hippie cool kids in ninth grade, most of whom were older, since I was usually the youngest kid in the class. Most important, I didn't care about anything anymore. When I lit that joint and drank that beer, the feeling of well-being, of warmth and genuine acceptance, of everything being all right with the world, flowed through me.

Soon I discovered I could make stoned people laugh.

A few weeks after I got high for the first time, a pretty girl in my class told me, "Ken, you're fucking funny as hell."

I'll never forget it. She was infamous for her tight jeans and tank tops and had always completely ignored me when she wasn't making fun of me. I was standing in the woods behind the school where the smokers and the partyers went to hang out and light up. I could see the cafeteria through the trees, and I told tight-jeans girl something that had happened earlier in the woods, and she laughed and laughed and laughed, throwing back her long reddish-brown hair, the green of the trees, the green of her eyes, the redbrick cafeteria behind us, all mixing together.

I had the eureka moment I had been waiting for all my life. I'd get high and make people laugh. A sense of humor I developed as a kid to entertain my mother, my uncle, my grandmother had finally found a purpose. I had studied my mother and absorbed some of her crack wit and razor-sharp putdowns. Her sense of humor improved while drinking martinis. Soon my ability to make people laugh improved while smoking weed.

My buddies and I dealt with teen angst by smoking pot; listening to the Grateful Dead, Led Zeppelin, and the Rolling Stones (how we cheered on Keith Richard's heroin-induced blood transfusions); and competitively pursuing the prettiest girls in school. Some of the other kids were put off by this artificial extension of the 1960s. The music scene going on then was punk, and that didn't appeal to my friends' mellow Quaker-hippie-affected ideals. Some of the other kids cared about their classes and studying, and some just didn't want to join in.

I had always enjoyed being the center of attention. In my experimental Rudolf Steiner elementary school, I was a personality to be reckoned with, starring in school plays and excelling academically. Then we moved to Hawaii, and I had no chance to receive the attention I deserved. I swore when I returned home that I was going to be a doer, not a watcher. It wasn't enough to be cool—I had to be the coolest. That's how I went from a Catholic school–mandated uniform of a white shirt and blue slacks in twelve months to a uniform of my own creation. By sophomore year, I was sporting a big blue hat with a wide brim similar to Tom Laughlin's in the 1960s counterculture judo movie *Billy Jack*; long, bushy brown hair; and a jean jacket with Jimi Hendrix sewed on the back by a girl I had a crush on.

In a little over ten years, being cool almost killed me. When I graduated from high school, the final school newspaper of the year gave senior predictions. Mine was "Will open a school for acting cool and own a fleet of Mercedes." When I read that, I thought I had made it. In my senior year, I had several girlfriends and was inducted into a "secret society." Its high coolness factor was based on smoking pot, being popular, listening to the right music, and being an excellent Ultimate Frisbee player.

All of my decisions were based on what was cool and what wasn't. I was a fair actor, but when I realized that the thespians at my high school weren't cool, I stopped trying out for plays. So I didn't pursue something that gave me genuine pleasure. Perhaps it was also because I couldn't take the risk of opening up, of revealing myself onstage.

My grades suffered, though I reeled in enough A's and B's to keep my mother off my back. I took the SATs hungover, the morning after I went to a keg party. No Kaplan classes, pre-SAT practice tests, or college visits in our family. Our family entertained people. We'd make them laugh, keep them happy. My grandmother, June Dunnington Grimes, had not been a physically affectionate mother, as I came to understand later in reading my mother's semiautobiographical books. But she was affectionate with me, and we had some kind of special understanding that circumvented my mother. My grandmother made me Halloween costumes, stuffed animals, and let me watch the *The Honeymooners* with her. She could do anything, she was magic, and her opinion meant a lot to my mother and my uncle. She was the only person left from their childhood. Their father had died when they were young; they had no living uncles or aunts and only a few cousins whom they rarely saw.

I knew I had reached the mountaintop in our small family when I would make my grandmother laugh and she would say, "Ken, you just slay me."

My sense of humor is exactly that of my mother (except I'm not as funny) or my uncle, a man with a veritable Ph.D. in humor. Their humor is situational and based on quick retorts. When my mother and uncle got together, hilarity was guaranteed. Some of it was fueled by alcohol—the telling remark, the verbal shiv to the ribs, sometimes to the person in the room (that took at least two martinis)—though more often gossiping about people long dead or far away. But it was always entertaining.

After I crossed the Rubicon, when I entertained, there was no stony gaze from drunk adults, no clink of martini glasses. We were in the woods behind school, at my friend's houses for keg parties, in cars passing joints while we turned up the radio, at rock concerts with the music blasting.

I enjoyed the passing of seasons in those woods, the honey-chestnut of the leaves in fall, the vibrant greens of spring, the spare gray branches swaying gently in the winter. You could party before school, during morning break, between classes, at lunch hour, and after school, smoking cigarettes or getting high. Clouds of smoke would emerge from "first log," where people gathered around an enormous log, with a trash can for cigarette butts. If you wanted privacy, you could saunter down to "second log," thirty feet away, to spark a bowl with a few friends. If you really wanted to get away from it all, you could wander down the path to the creek. People would argue the merits of various pipes and bowls, musicians we liked, and gossip about kids or teachers.

When Bob Marley died, my Ultimate Frisbee team climbed one of the largest trees in the woods and passed around joints in his honor. Once I moved on to my junior and senior years, I saw the younger kids smoking to fit in, saw them age right in front of me, some of the aging natural—there's an obvious difference between a thirteen-year-old and a sixteen-year-old—some of it induced by alcohol and marijuana. Pot opens people up and gives a community feeling, much more so than alcohol. You share pot in a way that you don't share beer or liquor. Pot makes you mellow and easygoing, as opposed to alcohol, which often switches on aggression. But frequent pot smoking aged me in a way that's hard to describe; it made me distant. Perhaps it was because I desperately wanted to be older than I was, to be accepted.

The need to be cool is a common driver of adolescents and can be expressed in many ways. My problem was that, almost immediately, pot smoking wasn't enough of a high. There were many times when I smoked so much pot it no longer worked: that I "smoked myself straight." I wanted, needed, to be even higher.

People argue that marijuana is a gateway drug to hard drugs, and I would have to agree. Tobacco was my original gateway drug. When I was twelve years old, chewing Copenhagen and Skoal— "A little dip will do ya"—gave me a wicked head rush. I quickly moved on to Marlboros. Pot took me on the same elevator ride up, even higher than tobacco. I wore that out, and the spent embers of the 1960s and early 1970s promised more with LSD, so I took that.

Try explaining to your mother that you can't talk right now because you're hallucinating and she's turned into a dragon. I was able to go to school for a week straight, chewing on the corners of hits of acid, maintaining a steady buzz. I functioned, went to class, and spaced off on how the trees looked or on the color of the sky, until I had a strange deteriorating sensation in my brain and body, and stopped.

Tenth grade was the garbage-head year, the year of living dangerously, of someone saying in the woods, "Give it to Ken, he'll smoke anything." I soon had a rep of being the druggie's druggie. Underclassmen I didn't know were greeting me with a cheery "Hi, Spent Ken!" I snarled at one of them once, "You haven't earned the right to call me that." I was horribly embarrassed. Was I such a burnout that kids I didn't even know were talking about me?

I forged on to speed, downers, quaaludes, mushrooms, and finally, the drug of choice of the 1980s, cocaine. By the time I graduated from high school, I had settled on marijuana and beer. Cocaine was too expensive, though always desirable as a high unto itself.

I trained for alcohol and pot like some high school athletes train for distance running. I kept a running tally of the quantity I consumed and would brag about it to friends while the older kids rolled their eyes. Woe to me if I threw up, for the taunting was vicious; puking on someone's rug or in their car would tab you as a "lightweight" or "totally uncool." From the beginning, I was determined to be cool and to handle the rapidly increasing amounts of chemicals I consumed.

Just as I was turned on to drugs by friends and older kids, I lived to turn on others. I'll never forget the pretty Dutch girl telling me in the woods that I was getting her high for the first time. I was giving her "her wings," just like my first time in ninth grade. It was a real feeling of accomplishment to pass on to her what had been so eagerly passed on to me.

Except, in my case, it almost killed me.

10

MG

Cache

When did I first start drinking alcoholically? At one of those University of Maryland football games where we sat in the stands and guzzled a combination of gin and grape juice that we called Purple Jesus? I don't think so, party girl though I turned out to be in my sophomore year. My freshman year was spent in getting good grades, probably because I didn't know many people.

My sophomore year was such a stereotype of university days, it's laughable. Fraternity parties, dances (formal dances, with evening gowns and gardenias), mugs of beer at Bernie's; hanging around a piano in a fraternity house, singing a mildly obscene version of "Coffee in Brazil"; Les Paul and Mary Ford's "How High the Moon" playing for the thousandth time while we crowded into one of the glass-enclosed listening cubicles in a record store on D.C.'s F Street; crawling in the dorm window after hours because otherwise we couldn't get by Mrs. G., our dorm's ubiquitous drill sergeant of a housemother. Getting drunk, nursing hangovers with pride as if a hangover were a badge. All of that college stuff.

Was it all of those back-office cocktail hours, the pitchers of martinis Mrs. D. shared with me? I don't think it happened there, either, the tip-off when drinking meant more than a good time. There was a point when it became a need more than a want, when it broke away from partying or those happy, rudderless hours in the back office. There was a point when Jim Beam and Gordon peeled themselves off the labels and came to sit down beside me.

I think the alcoholic drinking might have started with that innocent bottle of sherry I kept in the closet. It could have been Amontillado or Harveys Bristol Cream. We speak of a trigger—a drink that triggers a real thirst. That bottle of sherry might have been it.

Perhaps it sounds impossibly quaint—an English teacher with a bottle of cream sherry in the cupboard. This is the same person who was quaffing martinis in the back office of a hotel for years. Why didn't I keep a bottle of gin or vodka in the closet, for God's sake? Because I associated martinis with the back office. I was quite happy with the sherry.

I bet I was.

Sherry. Closet. Stash. *Cache.* That sounds less like a trigger than a gun with a silencer.

It was almost as if I hadn't been doing any drinking of note before then. When I started to teach at a college in Frostburg, Maryland, I rented a room in another teacher's house. I remember enjoying Sundays: I'd have breakfast up on the main street, at a restaurant that was at heart a diner and still is today.

It was during one of these Sundays, poring over the paper, when it occurred to me, My, it would be nice to have a drink. For some reason, I thought of sherry, which had never been a serious contender. Perhaps a serious contender would have worried me—I mean, that I would even think of a dry martini in these circumstances. Forthwith, I purchased a bottle of sherry.

That I secreted it in the closet should have been a dead giveaway. There wasn't any particular reason for hiding it, as I don't think the woman who owned the house was either a teetotaler or a snoop.

I was thirty or thirty-one when I started that teaching stint and rented the room, which meant I had a lot of happy drinking years behind me. Consequently, this apparent drinking novitiate of a glass of sherry with the Sunday *Times* puzzles me even now. It might have been merely practical: My room was hardly set up for mixing a martini. I can't picture the closet housing both gin and vermouth and a little dish of lemon twists, to say nothing of ice. That could have come only from the kitchen, and I'd hardly have tried sneaking in and tapping out an ice tray.

Maybe the sherry was a shield. An example of denial. I would guess—though this might be wrong—that there is a moment when one moves from drinking she could have stopped to drinking she couldn't. Many would disagree; many—A.A.? the clinic? the last hundred books written on alcoholism?—would say that alcoholics are born, not made. I think alcoholism takes an education. That I was destined to become an alcoholic, I very much doubt. By the time I took that teaching job and moved into that room, I'd say I'd earned a degree.

The BA came with the University of Maryland; the graduate degree in drinking from the University of Iowa. Those were a couple of dandy places to become an alcoholic, and perhaps they were practice for it, but the essential thing was missing: I had to have that drink.

Between the two came that bottle of sherry, there on the other side of the line.

Was the line there before I crossed it? I don't know.

11

MG

It's Five O'Clock *Somewhere*

There are many programs conceived of as alternatives to Alcoholics Anonymous, some of them supporting "controlled drinking," such as Moderation Management; others built on the idea of complete abstinence, such as Rational Recovery. One of the most notable differences between A.A. and Rational Recovery is that the latter firmly believes one can be cured without being propped up by a group of similarly addicted people.

There used to be Rational Recovery groups, but the group idea, which suggests support, was jettisoned, seemingly because the recovery in this school of thought must be bootstrap (though it's called something else). Dependence on others to keep you sober, they think of as a lifelong dependence. This is one reason they don't go along with a twelve-step program, since it encourages a lifelong connection.

Some proponents of Rational Recovery seem to believe that

A.A. is an evangelical body, that it is really about religion, not drinking, and that this organization is always looking for converts. Admittedly, I had a problem with the Lord's Prayer sometimes ending meetings, but it didn't say to me that I was witnessing the windup of a Sunday service. I simply thought it was a little hypocritical in the light of A.A.'s having no religious affiliation. Nothing was being stuffed down my throat (except the millionth cup of coffee). I'm sure some members convert, go back to their religion, or take up some creed. Some, though, see great harm in this, saying that you're not your own man (as if any of us are), that what you need is not coddling (that's rich! have they ever talked to a *sponsor*?), and what you need to do is stop your addictive thinking. Well, I'll queue up for that! I'd love to stop thinking that somewhere, it's five o'clock, but never where I am. My addictive thinking has less and less of a hold on me, until it's become fairly vaporous and I have to pump it up to get any good out of it—still, I'd like to stop it and certainly to *have* stopped it back in the day.

Addictive thinking is dwelling on the signs and signals that get and keep you drinking (like our minds hovering over Harry's Bar in Venice, for instance, and don't we wish we could?). I doubt that Rational Recovery advocates therapy, since therapy could wind up as a dependence on another person.

The "addictive voice" of Rational Recovery seems to me to be similar to the internal sentences of rational emotive therapy. This is a school begun by Albert Ellis, who coauthored a guide to rational living with his colleague Robert A. Harper. Its thesis (and I know this, since I was a client of Dr. Harper) is that one is not made unhappy by the actions of somebody or something else, but by the internal sentences we construct that insist we should respond as if these actions reflect truth. Your daughter, say, calls you a bitch, says she loathes you. Dr. Harper would say, "That's not your problem, it's your daughter's. You're making it your problem by listening to what you're telling yourself in your head: that you must be unhappy because of what your daughter has said." Rational emotive theory has a lot to do with this "must" reaction.

It would take near-heroic detachment not to react to your daughter, but what Harper says is probably true. By "react," he means you shouldn't *feel* desolated, since the words are hers, not yours. What you're likely doing, in this mental process, is *making* the words yours. What I found to be the only difficulty with this therapy is that it needs reinforcement (like all therapies), and that means going to the therapist. Either the therapist or your own constant policing of your responses to emotionally charged situations.

The internal sentences are like the addictive voice of Rational Recovery, The AV tells you you need a drink. You tell the AV, no, I don't. I imagine this dialogue continues for a while until one or the other voices cashes in its chips. What's the difference between doing this and the usual old stuff of telling yourself, I need a drink! No, I don't! Yes, I do! Don't drink! Drink!

People generally are driven not by reason but by emotion, so that "rational" behavior—i.e., "recovery"—has a very long row to hoe, in that you are supposed to be able, in the simplest terms, to talk yourself out of your addiction. I just don't see how you can.

How can you drink rationally? Rationality has nothing to do with drinking. Although a ton of books pressing for controlled drinking would disagree with me, I think there are only two kinds of drinkers: nonalcoholics and alcoholics. For the first group, "rational" as a word to define drinking is meaningless, simply because a social drinker, a drinker who is satisfied after a drink or two—drinking is not a problem. For the second group, "rational" didn't get you *to* where you are now, so why would it get you *out* of it? "Rational" is just another word in the service of "control." The nonalcoholic doesn't think about control. The alcoholic thinks about it all the time. It's what he's trying to do but can't.

Moderation Management is a program that would disagree with me because it believes that there are many drinkers who are only "problem drinkers" and who, if the problem is caught in time, can avoid addictive drinking. I think the person who believes he has a problem, really does. "I'm not an alcoholic, only a problem-drinker" sounds like a dangerous assessment.

Promises to oneself: "I won't drink until five"; "I'll stop for a week [a month, a year]." The point is not whether one keeps the promise but that one has to make the promise in the first place.

Let's say you can do it, that you can monitor your drinking, apportion the drinks to a few a day ("Ten beers and I'm outta here!"), that you can stop after one drink at lunch, or even stop drinking at lunch altogether, or allow yourself no more than three drinks—one an hour—at a party. Do you want to? Do you want to go through life having to police yourself, to undertake this kind of surveillance? What sort of deliverance from sobriety is that? I mean, three lousy drinks spaced out. The only thing worse is one or two, and that's unthinkable.

A good friend and fellow drinker, Leon, was told by a doctor that he would have to restrict himself to two ounces of alcohol a day, i.e., one decent martini. Leon's reaction was to say if that was all he could have, why not just stop altogether? Remarkably, he did. This is the same Leon who would meet me at the end of the driveway with a martini in each hand. (We had a contest going: Who could get the martini to the other person quickest?)

The trick is that it's better not to have the first one. It's the first that wakes everything up, like the little lights and raucous noise of a pinball machine.

For the person who is not addicted to chocolate, one truffle is satisfying. For an addict, well, just hand me the box and pretend we never met. For an alcoholic, there is no such measure as "one martini." One martini is a contradiction in terms.

Rational Recovery does not believe in alcoholism as a disease. A.A. does; accepting it as a disease is crucial to getting well. I don't care whether it is or isn't a disease; you have to take the same steps to overcome it.

A lot of A.A. dropouts take up some form of moderation. I would assume they do it because a lifetime without drinking is unimaginable—and, I'm sure they would add, unnecessary. But people who join groups to get *help* must feel they have a problem (well, an issue) with whatever the group espouses.

If you think, no, you're not an alcoholic, just someone who has a drinking problem, why not solve your own problem? You tell yourself you need to cut down. So cut down. But isn't that the problem? You haven't been able to do that. Thus, you hitch up with a program that's designed to let you keep drinking. Now, *that's* a program any alcoholic could live with!

There are obviously drinkers who can do it; if there weren't, the moderation groups would have gone out of business. There are also drinkers who can quit without attaching themselves to any group or organization. They can stop by themselves. It's harder. And it's rare.

If Leon did it—old drink-at-the-end-of-the-drive Leon, then maybe you can, too. But don't bet on it.

12

A Round of Pints, Please

Whatever I thought my future held changed the day I graduated from high school, when my mother had to pick me up from the local police precinct. I had been busted for drug possession with my girlfriend and two best friends. My aunt and uncle drove my mother. The shame I felt was overwhelming, and I cried endlessly when I got to my room in the basement.

That ended quickly. Even in my despair, I began to figure out how to get out of the situation. I had been caught, which was a drag, but I wasn't going to stop partying. I just needed to be more careful. So what if my mother had watched me receive my diploma or my uncle had hosted a graduation-day lunch for the family at his house? I was buzzed, cocky, and feeling superior to everyone. I was a happening guy who was going to college. My cousins weren't, poor bastards.

That feeling of entitlement quickly disintegrated. My arrest was combined with losing my driver's license and my girlfriend telling me that her father wouldn't let her see me anymore. My lawyer said I must get a summer job immediately, no matter how demeaning, to show that I was serious about cleaning up my act. I survived forty hours of community service at a YMCA swimming pool, by teaching mentally challenged kids how to play Frisbee. I tacked on to that a job of selling newspaper subscriptions door-to-door with some junior-high kids and our forty-year-old chain-smoking, van-driving, dentistry-challenged crew boss who was married to the best salesperson on our team—an eighteen-year-old blond girl who had run away from home. It was the worst job I ever had. We preyed upon old people who had no one to talk to and tried to sweet-talk them into multiyear subscriptions of a weekly newspaper that they clearly didn't need.

My attorney finally brokered a deal with the chief of police, who decided not to pursue any legal action against me. As a seventeen-year-old minor in an era when teenage drug possession was still relatively new, I received a slap on the wrist and was free to leave the state and attend college.

It was a long, hot, boring summer that culminated in a thirty-year-old guy beating me up at the park in front of my friends after an Ultimate Frisbee game. He was even more competitive than I was and kept jawing at me, so I decided to deliberately out-play him for kicks. He became so enraged that, after the game, he started punching me. I didn't fight back. None of my friends stopped him, they stood and watched. I ran to my car and wept as I drove myself home.

My mother could see that I was miserable and did her best to help. She asked if I was interested in leaving the U.S. and going back to England to work for her friend Charlie in London. He had called her to offer me a job working in the cake factory he managed in the North of England near Newcastle. She had vague intimations that Charlie was a "character," but what she didn't know was that Charlie was associated with the English mafia. They had met a few years earlier at one of the pubs she frequented while doing research for one of her mysteries.

I was in awe of Charlie. The previous Christmas, the three of us had tied on a hilarious drunk in London, where he regaled us with tales about his coterie of disreputable friends. I leaped at the chance to get out of the country and leave my problems behind. When I spoke to Charlie on the phone, I was able to put together, despite his thick Cockney accent, that he could get me a job at a factory he ran in northern England.

I had planned to attend the University of Iowa in the fall, but now I had some hazy notion that I would start the following spring. The week before I left for England, I got a telephone call from the admissions office, telling me they were looking forward to seeing me in the fall, wanted to sign me up for orientation, and needed to talk to me about student housing.

"Actually, I'm going out of the country this week, so I won't be there this fall. I'm planning on coming for the spring semester," I said to the man on the phone.

There was a pause on the other end. "Ken, when were you planning on telling us? School starts in eight weeks." I could tell this guy couldn't believe what he was hearing, and frankly, neither could I. It hadn't occurred to me to call and let the college know I wouldn't be showing up.

"Look, kid, we'll keep a spot open for you in the spring. Let us know in a few months if you still want to enroll." He hung up.

I was tempted to bring some weed with me to London because I knew it was not as plentiful there as in the U.S., but I decided that being on the wrong side of the law once in the past two months was enough. When I got off the plane at Heathrow and went through customs with nothing to declare, a customs guard looked at my passport and said, "Mr. Grimes, this way, please."

Always polite, the customs guards gave a running commentary as they searched my bag, went through every item I had, opened up my vitamins and counted them, checked my wallet, patted down my clothes, and had a guard dog sniff me and my belongings, all while asking my business, my age, where I was from, what I planned to do in the UK, and whom I knew there.

They escorted me to a holding cell with several shifty-looking undesirables. The customs guards were unimpressed that the only phone number and contact I had was Charlie's father, so they let me sweat it out while they went to call him and see if he knew me. I wondered if my being arrested the month before had put me on some kind of Interpol list, or if they just didn't like bleary-eyed American teenagers without parents or a school group to vouch for their intentions.

After letting me cool off for several hours, the customs guards came back, apologized for the delay, gave me my belongings, and pointed to the exit door.

Cockney East Side men had run organized crime in London for decades. Charlie had ties to these men. He convinced his boss, Peter, to hire me as a stock boy/forklift operator in a frozen food factory he owned up near Scotland. Peter was the real article, or at least he appeared to be. An organized-crime figure who had gone legit, Peter claimed to be related to one of the gang that pulled off the Great Train Robbery of 1963. Peter liked to curse, drink, and show off his money.

Charlie felt a connection to me that stemmed from his own knockabout youth. He wanted me to be his sidekick in northern England, where I was even more out of place than he was. He also wanted me to spy on the other employees to see who was stealing the frozen cakes and apple pies. Considering what they were paid, Charlie should have been happy they didn't steal the milk, eggs, and flour as well.

I loved England. I had lived there for six months when I was ten years old and had gone to school in Hampstead. I spent multiple summers there with my mother from the time I was eight until I was twelve. We visited countless stately homes, manor houses, castles, and museums, and drove through the countryside as it changed from calm to mysterious to forbidding. Those early, happy experiences in England had deeply affected me.

At the age of seventeen, all I wanted to do was drink pints and pints of Guinness and smoke pack after pack of John Player Special Black cigarettes. On a trip to Ireland several years later, I vaguely remember going to Trinity College to see the *Book of Kells* again—my mother had taken me there as a child—but what I really remember was how fresh the Guinness was in Dublin. I loved Guinness more than anything. The strike of the wooden match to light my cigarette. The hush in the darkened pub, the murmuring voices, and the light reflected from the mahogany walls. The dark, rich, bitter beer that slid down my throat like ice cream. Guinness was a spiritual experience.

Charlie arranged for me to move in with an ex-con nicknamed "Tiny" for his diminutive size. Tiny was about 140 pounds, with a lined, baggy face, and lived in a very tidy, small two-bedroom council row house with a TV and no backyard. He lived in a small town in northern England not too far from Newcastle. Tiny's fourteen-year-old glue-sniffing son, who lived with his teenage girlfriend in a nearby housing council flat and aspired to be on the dole, was a frequent visitor.

Tiny and his friends schooled me in how to drink like a man. I drank Guinness, bitter, ales, anything but lager (what we drink in the U.S.), which was considered a woman's drink, and no half-pints; those were for women as well. I quickly learned how to drink without throwing up or falling down.

Tiny was a very kind and gentle chap. Like most of the local men, he was unemployed and very much at peace with living on the dole. All of the manufacturing jobs that employed Tiny and his mates—the coal, auto, shipbuilding, and heavy-manufacturing jobs—had disappeared in the 1970s. Labour Party stalwarts and Margaret Thatcher haters, these men drank, argued, and fought among themselves constantly, particularly at the pub. The ones who were married cheated on their wives, or claimed they did. Masculinity was measured by how much you could drink and if you could fight. At my favorite pub on the tiny Main Street in the village there was a standard joke—"That's not sawdust on the floor, that's last night's furniture."

All through high school, I had worked very hard at drinking without throwing up. Alcohol was more difficult to purchase than marijuana for a teen in suburban America, but with the kegs and six-packs we successfully bought, I tried to figure out how to pace myself so I could drink a six-pack or more without puking in the woods or in somebody's parents' house.

To be in some remote village in the UK with very little to do but drink with some of the local teenagers didn't appeal to me.

Drinking with men five, ten, fifteen years older than I was fun. They accepted me, spoke to me as an equal. I had never drunk this way before. It was obvious my usual limit of six to eight beers would have to be raised. By the time I left England at the age of eighteen, I was a stone-cold alcoholic able to drink ten pints of beer in one stretch.

On any given day, everyone met at the first pub, prepared for a serious bout of two to three hours' drinking, minimum. For a Friday or Saturday night, the pubs closed at eleven P.M., so we gathered early after dinner, drank until the pubs closed, then went to someone's house to continue drinking. The drinks were bought in rounds: In a group of six, each man would go to the bar and order six full pints and return to the table with the tall, thick glasses that widened as they went up and filled to the very rim with a light dusting of foam. Back in the 1970s and 1980s, a pint was between eighty pence to one pound twenty pence, so the unemployed could still afford to get drunk. If women were present, it got more complicated—and expensive—since they weren't expected to pay.

British beer is not warm or even room temperature. It is cold. Not cold, in that fake Budweiser American-commercial way, but cool and delicious. After the beers were placed on the table, someone took out a pack of cigarettes and offered them around. Drinking the cool draft of strong ale with its careful mix of aged hops and barley, while smoking throat-crackingly strong cigarettes, was something I could do for hours and hours.

One night at the more upscale pub down the street from my usual haunt, a couple of friends from work joined me for a night of carousing. As the night progressed, I noticed one of our legendary fisticuff experts, "the Hulk," staring at us. An aging, unemployed bruiser with a head the size of a keg of ale, he kept glaring at us from across the bar. I knew he wasn't mad at me, but for some reason, he didn't like the look of my friends. He had grandly forced his beautiful young daughter to go on a date with me the first week I was in town, an embarrassment for both of us, since she had an unemployed boyfriend who kept her occupied when she wasn't working at the factory. I wisely kept my hands to myself, and although Hulk was disappointed that I couldn't dislodge his daughter's suitor, he appreciated me for being a gentleman about it.

As I saw the Hulk approaching us, fear shot down my spine. I was terrified he was going to headbutt them, known locally as a "Geordie hello." He asked my friends where they were from, and before they could reply, the Hulk grabbed one by the back of the head and slammed his own forehead into the guy's nose.

The blood exploded across both men, and everyone in the bar rushed up and kicked us outside. I stood in the doorway and looked at my mates and shrugged. They nodded and shuffled off. It was not an uncommon night.

What did I do the next night? Go out to drink, of course. The banter and the laughter of drinking companions in pubs made the hours roll by in countless amusing ways. My favorite was the man who would sidle up to me occasionally and ask what I was drinking and make me a challenge. "Aye, son, if you buy me onna them pints, I'll eat this glass right in front of yeah."

As a well-traveled, sophisticated partyer I doubted him the first time but ordered a pint of his favorite ale. He stood chatting with me and glancing over occasionally to a couple of the barflies, who were smiling, already on to the game.

After draining the glass, he slowly and calmly begin to eat it one bite at a time, carefully chewing and swallowing the pieces. My jaw dropped in astonishment, and he laughed.

"The hardest part is when the pieces get stuck in yah teeth in da back," he said proudly. "But this is nothing. You canna believe me when I chew a bottle of Newcastle Brown." Newcastle Brown ale was the good locally brewed beer, and the bottles were made of thick, brown opaque glass.

Alcoholism is measured not only in quantity of alcohol consumed or number of pint glasses eaten but also decisions made. For example, trying to date the most attractive woman at the factory where I was working. A frozen food factory is not high on the list of places to fall in love when you're seventeen, but how could I resist Julie? Though there were some very attractive women at the factory, Julie was the prettiest of them all, and she liked to come out back and flirt with the stock boys while catching a quick smoke. I soon found out that she was married to—but separated from—a much older man who had recently been let out of prison for stabbing someone in a fight.

Somehow that only made her more interesting.

The factory was a moldering behemoth in an industrial park on the outskirts of town, a relic of the complete collapse of the manufacturing era. The nearest city of any size was Newcastle, which was still suffering from the strikes and mass layoffs of the 1960s and 1970s.

I've noticed that the only people—writers, academics, Republicans—who extol Henry Ford's invention of the assembly line are people who've never worked on one. I suppose automated production of everything from cars to cakes changed the world for the better, but stand on your feet for eight hours with a thirty-minute break and two fifteen-minute cigarette breaks, doing the same monotonous task over and over, every day, every week, and you'll wonder about progress.

The women on the various product lines made the best of it, calling out to one another in their singsong Geordie accents while listening to a radio perched high overhead, tuned in to the local hit parade. I have every English pop hit from the fall of 1982 memorized, particularly the Human League's "Don't You Want Me," which seemed to play every fifteen minutes.

As a stock boy in the frozen cake section, I got to wear a spiffy blue jumpsuit and white boots, like a reject from David Bowie's "Major Tom" video. I was charged with operating a forklift, moving huge metal canisters of milk into the cold room, and stocking fifty-pound bags of white flour. The factory made frozen apple pies for one high-end supermarket chain and a gâteau for a moderate-priced market chain. Their use of the French word for cake always amused me, because there was nothing French about those cakes.

When you're seventeen, it's a rush learning how to move five-hundred-pound pallets on a giant forklift. And nothing could be cooler than operating the machine and scouring the workplace to find the most attractive woman in the company. Why? Because only the unreachable, the unattainable, would move my levers. I knew it was dangerous at the time, in that half-understood way of teenagers, but I didn't care, because once Julie started flirting with me, I would have picked up a five-hundred-pound pallet with my hands. As the only American there, I had instant celebrity. I think everyone at the forsaken place lived within a ten-mile radius of the factory, and very few had even been to London, which was three hundred miles away.

Julie was a froster, the glamour job at the factory. She wore her cute white hat cocked at a jaunty angle while working a big white bag of frosting, twisting it rapidly in her hands to create the various designs on top of the gâteaux.

The interior of the factory was not well lit, and there was a constant hum and crash of motors wheeling the foods around the line. Charlie, the lord of the realm, stayed behind large plate-glass windows near the main entrance and liked to stare at the workers. Pretty girls he fancied or male workers he took a liking to were invited to drink Smirnoff vodka in the back room. I was one of those favored. I never liked vodka as a teenager. It was my mother's drink, my uncle's drink, served in a big glass pitcher with ice and refrigerated until the pitcher was whisked out and drinks were poured into crystal glasses. Vodka smelled bad and tasted worse. But ah, the effect. Vodka worked faster than beer, made me warm inside, and promised instant friendship with those I drank with.

Charlie was the master of the drunken joke and regaled us with anecdotes about the peculiar inhabitants of the town and of his former haunts in the East End of London. As is true of many Cockneys, Charlie was a natural storyteller and loved to hold court with his captive employees, who would listen to anything for a chance to take a break from work, sit down, and have a free drink.

Charlie liked to pull me off the factory floor and send me to buy his vodka at the off-license down the road from the factory. He would hand me a twenty-pound note and tell me, "Ken, a quart of Smirnoff, and mind how you go."

Glad to be pulled out of the stockroom to do something useful, I would jump on the rickety old bike someone had left at the factory and pedal furiously down to the shop, buy the vodka, and race back. One day I trotted back to Charlie's office, fresh from a sortie to the liquor store. A small crew had already gathered, waiting for the delivery. As I handed Charlie the bag, it slipped in passing. The bottle crashed to the floor, and the vodka splattered everywhere, filling the room with a medicinal smell. Charlie looked at me in horror and yelled, "My God, boy, go back for another one! Here's another twenty quid, and don't fucking break it this time."

In a matter of weeks, it was obvious to Charlie that I had something going with Julie. We would sneak outside and make out during our breaks, and people began to talk. Charlie told me not to touch Julie and warned me not to switch from the daytime shift to the four-to-midnight shift to follow Julie, who changed her shift. But I didn't listen. Her husband was nicknamed "Stevie" because he, too, wore large, darkly shaded glasses like the famous pop musician. Everyone feared him, even the best of the pub fighters. Even though he and Julie were separated, he wouldn't take kindly to his wife dating anyone, particularly not some American teenager.

Julie and I would eat our lunch together at eight P.M. in the break room next to the men's locker room. The ceilings and walls were stained brown from the cigarette smoke. About 80 percent of the women smoked, and even more of the men. Our eight-week romance—which was never consummated and consisted of furtive visits on park benches in front of run-down council flats, where we would make out and talk—was fated to end in ruin, because in a small town, everyone knew everything about one another. People were certainly watching me.

Our friendship became public with a visit to the local disco in a down-market mall nearby. You had to be a paying member to enter this penultimate 1980s nightclub, where strobe lights flashed and winked in time to the throbbing music. Julie and I went with a friend of hers who was a member. We drank and drank and started to move closer and closer together. When Julie's favorite song—a remake of "Can't Take My Eyes Off of You" by the Boys Town Gang—started playing, she grabbed me and swung me out onto the dance floor, where we started to kiss. Although we were partially hidden by the other working boys and girls gamely shuffling in time to the music, I could see Julie's friend looking at us. When I walked back to our table, she shook her head and said, "Ken, you canna do this; Julie's still married, and Stevie will kill you if he finds out." I laughed and brushed it away, high off of the beer, the music, and Julie.

One night a week later at the factory, one of the women on the cake line burst into the break room. I could hear through the plate-glass windows overlooking the factory and realized there was a commotion coming from the assembly line. The woman said, "Ken, he's here, Stevie's here. He's screaming for the American and says he's going to kill yah. You must run now, he's coming up the stairs."

I hesitated. To run would be instant shame in any culture, much less he-man Geordie country. Julie turned to me and whispered, "Run, get out of here, I'll take care of Stevie."

I could hear him stomping up the stairs, yelling that he was "going to kill that bloody Yank." I ran to the back door and down the steps two at a time. I flung open the corrugated metal door at the back of the factory and emerged into the amber night sky of the parking lot.

I sprinted across the parking lot, the lights of the factory growing dim, my blue jumpsuit blending in with the dark, my white boots whistling through the knee-length heather. I ran back home to Tiny, praying that he would know how to save my life.

Tiny listened calmly as I told him what had happened. We sat in the dark of his living room, both of us chain-smoking. He would get up occasionally to move the curtain and see if Stevie had followed me home; everyone knew where I lived. Tiny told me not to worry, he'd take care of things. I could see in his eyes that he understood; he didn't lecture me about how stupid I was. He seemed to remember what it was like to be seventeen.

Recovery programs suggest you make amends to those you've harmed and ask for forgiveness. Only once have I made amends in a men's bathroom in front of urinals in a murky haze of cigarette smoke. That's what Tiny arranged the next week. He made me swear I'd stop seeing Julie, and he promised to broker peace between me and Stevie.

There I was, a few nights later at the pub, quaffing one pint after another, trying to keep away the terror that filled me as I imagined Stevie finding me and killing me. Then Tiny crept up to me and told me to meet him in the men's room.

It was dark, and the urinals stank and leaked their constant water, and I was unable to see Steve's eyes behind his dark glasses. I lied about chasing after his wife, and I tried to be convincing when I said I'd never see her again. He just stared at me, maybe with pity, maybe disgust, it was hard to say. We shook hands, and then I went back to drinking.

I lied. Nothing was going to stop me from seeing Julie. We made a last attempt to see each other for a weekend getaway to Scotland. I packed a suitcase and told Tiny I was going away to see a friend in London. I booked a hotel room in Edinburgh and took one of the run-down public buses up to Newcastle to meet Julie at the train station.

The station was enormous, and I waited at the ticket booth for over an hour, becoming more and more agitated. They began to call off the train number for the departure to Edinburgh. Like Humphrey Bogart in *Casablanca*, I searched for Julie's face among the passengers but couldn't see her blond hair or upright, confident stride anywhere.

The minutes ticked by. In desperation, I called her mother's house, since I couldn't call her at Stevie's flat. No answer. I kept dropping the coins in the pay phone, over and over, ringing again and again, until her mother came on the line.

"May I speak to Julie, please?" I asked, trying to modulate my voice and not sound like an American.

Her mother responded immediately, "You have to stop calling here, yoong man. Julie canna get away wit you, she told me to tell you that."

I dropped the phone, picked up my beaten leather overnight bag, and took the bus back. I walked to a fancy pub at the end of the street that I rarely patronized. I had told everyone at my regular pub about my plan to be in London, and I didn't want to explain why I was back, bag in hand.

I opened a pack of cigarettes and started drinking and didn't stop for the next three hours. Although I was embarrassed and ashamed, it felt good to be in the pub. Quiet. Alone. And drinking. I sat on the overupholstered couch, watching the smoke drift upward. The pub was empty, the afternoon light leaden and heavy.

Days later, Charlie switched me from the night shift back to the day shift. I endured the humiliatingly compassionate looks from my coworkers as the news spread instantly from shift to shift. Later that week, I waited for Julie for hours at the bus stop between shifts, hoping she'd show up. When I finally saw her walking to the factory entrance, she refused to turn around and look at me, even though she knew I was standing there.

It was a cold morning and a long walk home.

13

MG
—

It's Impossible

I got a call from Western Union: "Regarding the money you wired to a Ken Grimes in Iowa City, Iowa?"

"Yes."

"Well, the person who took the message made a mistake; he thought you were wiring five hundred instead of fifty."

"That's impossible."

"No, ma'am." He apologized profusely for Western Union. "But your son," he said, "collected five hundred. So could you please make up the difference?"

Ken had called and asked me to send him fifty dollars for books he needed for one of his classes. Why did it have to be wired, though? I suppose he rooted through his bag of reasons and pulled out something equivalent to an emergency room's "code blue" for books.

That was a week before I talked to Western Union. I put down the phone, appalled, not just that Western Union could have committed such a gross error but that Ken could have collected the money and said nothing. It's impossible. No, it isn't. No, it wasn't. So I called him. Finding Ken at the University of Iowa was like chasing down one zebra in a herd rushing across the Serengeti Plain.

Finally, we connected. "I'm sorry, Mom." His plaintive voice. "I thought you were really sending me five hundred."

"What? How could you think that?"

Can you hear a shrug? "I guess I just did."

(Lie.)

I'm sure he apologized at least as much as Western Union, abjectly.

Fast-forward a few years, after he has his degree, after he's stopped drinking and drugging. I bring up this five-hundred-dollar debacle. And now I hear the real reason:

"I was stoned out of my mind; I didn't know what was going on; I convinced myself that you sent five hundred; you were just being generous or something."

It's every mother's lament: I didn't know he was doing all those drugs. At least not so much as to cause this kind of distortion in his thinking. He couldn't work out the math? No. Being stoned, he could, through some exercise in quantum mechanics, make fifty turn into five hundred.

Any addict's "reason" for doing something is possible, because reason doesn't apply. Trying to reason with an alcoholic is like trying to argue with gravity. You're like Sisyphus, pushing that huge rock up that high incline only to have it fall back. You push again, and it falls back again.

We all respond irrationally much of the time. We like to think we're rational human beings when we are, in fact, driven by emotions, not reason. We're driving, rushing at a wall, though some of the time we can jam on the brakes.

All of this is exacerbated by drugs and drink. Addicts live in a wonderfully elastic world that expands and contracts at their bidding, where the laws of gravity don't apply. They can fly away.

I always loved that song of Perry Como's "It's Impossible." It's probably well loved by addicts, too. If you asked one for the world, somehow he'd get it.

Or say he would.

That was one phone call.

Then there was the phone call from the dean of students at the University of Iowa, where Ken had been in sketchy attendance for three years, informing me that they couldn't find him.

I stared at the telephone. I even shook the receiver a few times, thinking perhaps the voice would fall out and explain the prank.

"What do you mean, 'can't find'?" Idiots. How had they lost him in the first place?

"He hasn't been to his classes in a couple of weeks."

This was one of the scariest moments of my life. I had a picture of the whole university mounting a manhunt, sniffing dogs and all. That having failed, they were now driven to call the parent.

The dean went on, "And he hasn't paid his tuition."

Money I had sent him long before.

I don't recall what else was said. Probably not much. Not from my end, certainly; I was too shocked to say anything. Perhaps I should have realized that a student not showing up for classes and spending tuition money on other, more vital things, such as beer, wasn't that unusual.

Totally unnerved, I called my brother, who lived in Olney. He called the police in Iowa City. He then offered (as only Bill would) to go out there himself and see what he could do. But we waited to see what happened.

It happened fairly quickly. All the police did was go to Ken's address (something the university authorities couldn't figure out to do?), where he was, in the same place he'd been living all along with several friends. It was Ken, said the pleasant policeman, who came to the door. He was all right. We told him to call.

Did the policeman tell me he was drunk? Stoned? I don't think so. He was, of course, but I don't think that was mentioned.

Ken had his excuses, naturally. If he could have printed them up and put Lincoln's face on each one, we'd be rich. He was a buffet of excuses. They were heartfelt.

Tell a baby not to cry. It's just impossible.

Why was Ken at the University of Iowa in the first place? Considering the schools within a stone's throw (Johns Hopkins not the least of them), Iowa was a strange choice, indeed. It was over a thousand miles from Maryland, very hard to get to except by car, if you didn't run out of gas. Which I did a couple of times, being near-penniless and running on fumes.

We had been living in Maryland for most of our lives. Why not the University of Maryland? He didn't want to go there; he wanted to get away. And twenty-five years ago, the University of Maryland wasn't the school that it is now.

I can think of no really good reason why he was in Iowa. I can think of a lot of reasons he shouldn't have been, not least of which is that for a college freshman, a thousand miles from home is a long, long way (even for those who valiantly assert that no distance is quite far enough).

The reason he went to Iowa was that I went there.

I think I saw Ken, in my mind's eye, sitting in that circle of writers, showing off his superb poetry or short story (where did that come from?), bonding with fame. I think I was trying to relive it all through him. This I might say was the real reason, but for an alcoholic, no reason is clear enough to be the real reason. It's funny how long you view a scene through a cocktail glass before you realize you're at very watery definitions.

It occurred to me too late, as too many things do, that I wasn't at Iowa as an undergraduate, and that's a qualitative, not a quantitative, difference. Undergraduates and grad students? Apples and oranges, not apples and bigger apples. Those are different worlds. And I was a teaching assistant, even farther from the tree.

I had applied for teaching positions at several universities (back in the days when a person could not only get a job but actually choose the job she wanted). I went for several interviews: Colorado, Iowa, and some college in New England. I chose Iowa. I'm not sure why—I was impressed by the person who interviewed me, by the campus, by the teaching load.

I found a small apartment in Iowa City of which I was quite proud. There was an icebox in the kitchen, the ancient kind with a door on the outside into which a turn-of-the-century iceman shoved a block he had hacked from a bigger block. It seems mythical to me now. I put big packages of ice cubes in it for parties. Of which there were many, and a large number of fellow teachers and graduate students to host or attend them.

For a housewarming, I held a painting party. We painted the living room red and the small foyer black. Picture that.

We loved it.

We were poets.

We were drunk.

Rather, they were poets; I was drunk.

I had never written poetry or anything else. But given that my friends were poets, I applied and was admitted to the poetry workshop, probably because they were in it. Not just anybody could get into Iowa's poetry and fiction workshops. I wrote a few lukewarm poems, which, to my surprise, some of the others liked.

I can't envision a lovelier tableau: the best writing workshop in the country and wonderful friends, talented friends. These poets were very serious about it and very good. A handful even then were well known, and others were on the cusp of fame: Don Justice, Philip Levine, Bob Mezey, Peter Everwine, Theodore Holmes, Henri Coulette, Knute Skinner. Fifty years later, lines of their poems, even whole poems, run through my head. They were that memorable.

The intellectual milieu was dizzying. And the parties and the bourbon and the gin. It was at times the stereotype of a bunch of young writers on the MGM lot. It was almost *A Moveable Feast*, for who needed Paris when we had Iowa City? Midwestern, staid, dry except for beer, but we always had Rock Island, Illinois, if we wanted to drink.

Even as I write this, I know I've misremembered. The whole-sale exuberance should be a clue; the stereotype of the Young Writer, especially the Young Poet, should be another.

We were intense, we were talented, we were talk talk talk.

It was no place to send a kid who'd shown signs of poor judgment, one being graduation night from his favorite school and its back woods.

Naturally, there was a party.

Naturally, there were beer, pot, cocaine.

Naturally, there were police.

This time they called me.

Here was yet another telephone stare, another moment of impossibility, another of life's scariest moments, another call to my brother. I wouldn't have called, but I needed transport to the police station, since I'd let Ken have the car for the graduation party. Lucky car. It was being held, too.

He was being held not just for ingestion of an illegal substance but also for distribution. The idea was ludicrous, but I wasn't laughing at the duty sergeant who delivered the news. I could just hear his self-satisfaction thrum, as if no news were more delight-ful to unload than bad news about a stoned or drunk teenager. Had the substance ingested been air, they'd have made it stick. So there came another of life's impossible, dreamlike, this-can't-be-happening moments.

Driving back with my brother and sister-in-law in their car, I wondered what had happened. Not very productive, perhaps, but I couldn't help it. There were recriminations coming from the front seat. I wasn't really into that, sitting in the backseat with Ken, who was as silent as stone.

I think at such times it sweeps over a parent, any parent: What happened? A rush of memories of that little person at two and five and eight, wreathed in smiles, in little-guy joy, now sitting in big-guy misery and silence.

All of us could be flinging blame right and left, maybe because that makes us feel more secure in some weird way—the idea that there is blame to bestow. My question was, was it somehow inevitable that this happen? My answer was yes. Not this, precisely, but something like it, less or more, but something. There's no way to sidestep it or explain it. I could blame me, blame him, blame the woods behind the school, blame his pot-smoking, party-loving friends, but it's nothing like that, or it's everything like that. Say the parents, say society, say everything.

It's impossible.

14

—

The Flimflam Man: How Shakespeare Saved My Life

I admired crooks and liars as a kid. They knew what they wanted, and they took it. As a kid watching the musical *Oliver!*, I identified with the Artful Dodger and Fagin, not Oliver. I lied a lot growing up, and the more I lied, the more convincing I became. I quickly learned that I had to lie to party the way I wanted to.

Money was scarce when I went to college. My father made a modest salary and couldn't contribute much to my college education. So my mother ended up footing most of the bill, and she assumed that when I asked for tuition money, it would be spent on tuition. I had no idea how much money I needed or how to budget or pay bills. I was always running out because I spent it all on drinking.

My favorite T-shirt in college said, "What Do You Mean I Ran Out of Money? I Still Have Checks Left." I wrote checks for anything and to everyone, including my dealers. How stupid is that? This behavior couldn't be more different than what my mother and father did. My mother put herself through college by working for the federal government and as a teaching assistant at the University of Maryland. My father borrowed from relatives and took out loans. Not me. I couldn't have cared less.

Early in my freshman year, I found myself without any cash and desperate to fill my weed and beer habit. So I did what generations of college kids have done. I called my mother and asked her for money—fifty dollars, wired immediately. When she asked why I needed the money so quickly, I said I had to buy books and talked her into going to Western Union that day.

For the promise of free beer and weed, my friend Stan volunteered to take me to Western Union. We jumped into his green Plymouth Barracuda and peeled out of the dorm parking lot while huffing a joint. Stan dropped me off and kept the engine running while I rolled up to the counter at Western Union.

"Hi, my name is Ken Grimes, and I'm here to pick up a wire in my name."

The kind midwestern woman behind the counter said, "Yes, let me check."

She went to a room in the back and emerged with an envelope. "Here it is—a wire for five hundred dollars."

My mind began to race. I coughed, cleared my throat, and said, "What was that? Five hundred dollars?"

She looked quizzical. "Yes, isn't that correct?"

"Ah, that's right." I reached out to take the envelope stuffed with twenty-dollar bills. Trying to control my smile, I walked slowly out the door and then ran to the car. "Quick," I said to Stan, "let's get the hell out of here before they figure it out." We felt victorious and couldn't wait to start bingeing as soon as possible.

A semilogical mind might have followed this whole sequence: My mother had wired fifty dollars; Western Union gave me five hundred dollars; Western Union was out four hundred and fifty dollars, and they would want it back. But I needed money for booze. For me, that was the end of the story.

Western Union eventually figured it out. They contacted my mother and demanded payment. For a teacher earning twenty-eight grand a year, merely sending me to college was hard work. To receive a bill for an added five hundred was too much.

When I came home for spring break, my mother accosted me about the money. "Ken, what were you thinking? How did you do it? Where did you think the money was going to come from?"

As usual in these situations, I mumbled a reply, flailing wildly and turning the tables to make it her fault. "I don't know, I mean, I thought you said you were going to send fifty dollars, that's what I thought. It's Western Union's fault—they had the money order for fifty dollars but gave me five hundred!"

We fought, with me bobbing and weaving back and forth faster than Muhammad Ali. We came to no conclusion because I couldn't pay her back, I had no money. She threatened that I would have to get a job at school, something I fought tooth and nail to avoid. I wanted to party and get fucked up, not work like my mother, father, uncle, and practically everyone else from my parents' generation.

I had worked enough when I was a kid, from my first job at age eight, selling greeting cards door-to-door to all of the five A.M.

paper routes; mowing and raking the neighbors' yards; summers spent painting houses; teenage years working all manner of odd jobs. I just wouldn't do it anymore.

Working would cut into my drinking time, and that was sacrosanct.

The first day of classes in my sophomore year (I can't remember which class, since I dropped it shortly thereafter), the teacher decided to do one of those fake-intimacy exercises where we sat in a circle and introduced ourselves, then revealed one thing we wanted most out of the class and college in general.

I had a vicious hangover. I knew I was going to hate this class and my classmates. After a full round of pious statements, one student said, "I want to learn the most I can in the class and really learn something about life."

It was finally my turn. I looked blankly at them and said, "My goal is survival."

The teacher and the rest of the students stared at me. In that one moment, I had actually meant what I said. I was so depressed that survival was all I could hope for, and they knew I was telling the truth.

I remember my college girlfriends and some of our drunken revelry. After I broke up with one girl whom I had met at a party, she said, "You know, Ken, all those months we were together? We were drunk every single time we went home."

I just nodded and drank some beer out of my cup and played it off. I knew there was something wrong with that. I just didn't want to think about it.

I laughed and drank in the company of my friends, drank even more in the company of strangers, and drank depressed and alone more than I care to remember. I was one of T. S. Eliot's "Hollow Men," with a headful of straw. I was wasted, wasting my time, with no direction and no hope.

I knew my life would go out with a motherfucking bang, not a whimper.

Two years later, in the fall of my senior year, I was reading Shakespeare's *Henry IV,* Part 1, and I realized that I, too, could make it out of the college bars and taverns, the endless keg parties, the depressing exchanges with drunken teenagers. I sat in the smoking section of the college library and puffed one Marlboro Light after another. Suddenly, I felt a sense of hope. If Prince Hal could forswear Falstaff—and who in his right mind could resist Falstaff?—then maybe I could resist the nonstop boozing and waking up with no idea where I had been or what I had done.

I decided to improve my grades and get out of this shithole college town with a grade-point average that might get me a job. In a black spiral notebook, I created a chart of how many times I smoked cigarettes, smoked pot, drank beer, went to class, how many hours I studied, and all of it in a secret code in case one of my friends read it. I was terrified of being ridiculed. I noticed that when I went to class, studied, and didn't drink too much during the week, my grades improved. In my senior year, I pulled off a 3.6 GPA, made the dean's list, and ended up with an overall 3.01 GPA.

Years later, I was in the wedding party of one of my few college friends. We started talking about old times, and one of the gang reminded me that as a senior, I had schooled him—a piddling sophomore—on how to party correctly. As we sat at this college-reunion bender masquerading as a wedding, my only defense against everyone else's constant consumption of vodka, beer, and pot was the smoke from my cigars (I ended up smoking so many that I made myself sick).

My ex-sophomore friend—nicknamed "Hospital Balloon" for some forgotten reason that indicated a prodigious appetite for alcohol and drugs—said, "Yeah, man, don't you remember? You told me that night in the library: 'This is how it's done. You go to your classes—at least most of them. You come in here every night after class and study for two hours. Then you go out and rage on the weekends!'"

I had no recollection of that conversation. Once sober, I couldn't remember most of those years. I'm envious when my wife gets together with her college friends and they reminisce about their time at the University of Virginia. Occasionally, they drank too much; sometimes they went to football games; they attended sorority and fraternity parties, chased boys, went to class, and had a good time. My wife's friends went on to study in graduate school and work and find husbands and have productive lives. No guarantee of happiness but a decent shot at it.

In my college years, there were many times when I would lose my voice from twelve hours of smoking and drinking. First it would get raspy, then I could barely speak. This happened to many of my friends during binges. My best friend from college, my main man, now lives a shadow life. We were such good friends in college that we could end each other's sentences. We each knew what would make the other laugh—even if he wasn't around—and would save up stories to tell each other later.

Five years ago, he nearly died of congestive heart failure at forty-one. Now he suffers from Wernicke-Korsakoff syndrome, a form of wet brain that has left him unable to work. He has peripheral-vision problems and difficulty following linear thought patterns. Another friend destroyed his marriage and moved to Las Vegas, where he works as a bill collector. Some others are stumbling through their forties in an alcoholic haze. A few of them made it out alive.

I vaguely remember Big 10 football games where we stormed the field after big wins or wrestled one another in the stands to grab the "peace pipe" of pot whenever it stopped circulating because someone was hogging it. Or coming home from the games to take a "football nap" so we could go out to the bars and party until one A.M., then come home to drink until four A.M. The next morning I would find bruises on my body that I couldn't explain. I ate so much goddamned late-night pizza that, to this day, I hate pizza. I stopped playing Ultimate Frisbee or engaging in any other form of exercise and gained too much weight.

I wasn't alone. There were thousands of teenagers doing the same thing any given night. Some of them were alcoholics in the making, but most of them were not. They didn't leave a fun party in the living room to hide and snort coke in the back room. They didn't look out the window at nine A.M. on a Sunday, after a twenty-four-hour jag, to see people going to church and wonder what it would feel like to be normal.

At the end of senior year, my gang went on a weeklong bender to celebrate graduation. My mother and father and other relatives made the trek out to the Midwest for my special day. I graduated with the worst hangover I ever had in my life and was desperate for the ceremony to be over and for them to leave so I could start partying again. College was another crowning achievement in my life ruined by alcohol and drugs. Somehow I got out with a degree. Through my mother's editor, I got a job in book publishing in New York City.

Then the real fun began.

15

Double *Double Indemnity*

"Straight down the line, Walter."

Another member of our group is leaving. He's standing before us, giving reasons for his decision to stop coming to the clinic. They're pretty much the same reasons. Or reason: He has his drinking under control now.

Straight down the line, Walter.

That's more or less what I want to say to him. It's what Phyllis (Barbara Stanwyck) says to Walter (Fred MacMurray) in that great film noir *Double Indemnity*.

In any well-constructed mystery, there is a sense of inevitability. In most cases, the reader realizes it only after the last page is turned: *Of course, how could it have been otherwise? Double Indemnity* ratchets forward like a bullet out of a gun. You can't squeeze it back in; you can't turn it or dodge it. The target will be struck. And the target is them.

The movie begins with a gorgeous romance into which is interjected something chancy and dangerous, thereby making the romance even more glamorous. Then they do the dangerous thing together, and it's all downhill from there. What's especially damning is the corrosive agent in their love. What's eating at them is not so much guilt as the awareness that, having committed this crime, they're stuck with each other.

I've watched *Double Indemnity* so many times that I think it's leaking out of my pores as slowly as my last drink. It's such a beautiful piece of chiaroscuro; the lighting should be distilled and drunk neat. There's the scene at the end where she's sitting in her living room, waiting for him with a gun; his shadow is thrown on the wall as he stands in the doorway with a gun. They didn't go all the way together; they stopped and shot each other. Crash.

Straight down the line, baby.

Straight down the line.

After that earlier dialogue, you think, Oh, God! Now it's come to this!

And "this" is where I see our own Walter, announcing he's quitting.

The way in which *Double Indemnity* moves along the track to its inescapable end is the way this fellow will end. He can handle his drinking. He's got a plan. Say, drinking only on weekends. It doesn't matter. What he's thinking about now is the taste of that first drink.

Crash.

He's Walter. The bottle's Phyllis. They're a perfect fit. The bottle is alive with solace and the fulfillment of desire. So was Phyllis for two thirds of the film.

There is no stop on this train ride until you're over the rail and onto the track, like Phyllis's husband.

There is another reading of "straight down the line."

If this member of our group is anything like me, that first drink, that taste, is as good as a kiss, a long embrace and the return of a flaming romance. That first drink, and it all unravels. Not immediately, but give it time, until a drink later he realizes he's stuck with it. It's straight down the line for both of them, and neither one can get off, and the last stop (says Walter's boss) is the cemetery.

When you're in the "Surely one drink won't hurt" frame of mind, don't stop with imagining the first taste of that first drink. Imagine the second drink. Imagine the third. The fourth. At what point does the memory of that first lush icy taste on your tongue disappear and you start, well, just drinking?

What has kept me sober is that I know I can't drink just one. That sounds stodgy; it sounds boring; it's unimaginative. It would sound so much nicer, more romantic or sentimental, to say it's the love of my grandchildren that keeps me sober. It isn't. Nor is it my health; nor is it writing. It's knowing I can't drink just one. I go straight down the line with two, three, four until I see myself over the rail and onto the track. I know it would happen.

Crash.

In *Double Indemnity,* there's no strenuous drinking (although they don't exactly miss a chance). When Phyllis happens to have only a pitcher of iced tea handy, he drinks it, says, "A little rum would get this up on its feet."

My sentiments exactly, Walter. Up on our feet until we all fall down.

Crash.

16

MG

Throw Me from a Train, Please

One of my favorite movie scenes is the opening of *Throw Momma from the Train*. Billy Crystal plays a writer with severe writer's block. His ex-wife has stolen his book idea and is famous because the book is a best seller. He stares at his typewriter (how pleasant to see this relic) and tries desperately to get beyond the three words he has written. He stares out the window; he paces around the room, reciting the three words over and over; he makes himself a cup of tea and spends endless minutes dipping the tea bag in and out of the cup; he adds a shot of whiskey to the tea; he finally tries Scotch-taping his nose toward his forehead.

I don't know if I've ever had writer's block. In my drinking years, I would tell myself I had it. I could not come up with a sentence. I would stare at a blank page that remained irretrievably blank, not the temporary blankness through which I could see or sense a word or two but a blankness beyond blankness. My mind felt as if it were trying to navigate broken rocks barefoot. I didn't try the Scotch-tape trick.

What I wanted was easeful thought, smooth and seamless. What I got was a blank page that stayed blank while my mind was busy with the dinner menu.

After thirty years of writing books, my mind still resists. At times it appears to begrudge me every word I try to set down.

There I was with, say, fifteen books written, and I could still scare myself into thinking the fifteenth (or twelfth or seventh) could be my last book. Writing has always been precarious for me, but back then it was an utter cliff-hanger.

Rarely did I drink while I wrote. That's not because I was being a good little writer but because I wrote in the morning and I didn't drink in the morning. (When I did write in the evening, I would certainly keep company with a martini.)

The difference in the writing between my drinking life and my nondrinking life was not in output. I insist that one can write even when one can't (a seeming tautology). I'm all for putting words— any words—down on paper and worrying about them later. "Never, never, never walk away" was my motto.

What was the first book I wrote after I stopped drinking? I think it was *Rainbow's End*. I have a clear memory of Richard Jury sitting on the roof of the La Fonda Hotel in Santa Fe with a local policeman, engaged in the Santa Fe ritual (not quite as flamboyant as the Key West ritual) of watching the sun go down. I recall most clearly that everybody up on that roof out in the crisp New Mexico air was drinking.

It might seem to anyone who read the books from both parts of my life that they were pretty much the same (just as good or just as bad). Again, there was no difference in output. Consequently, one might wonder (and believe me, I did) what advantage lies in my not drinking.

It's one thing to stare down at a blank page and try to formulate a sentence—anything just to write—and not be able to (correction, thinking I wasn't able to), and conclude: That's it, I'm done for, I'm finished as a writer. It's quite another to see an unformed sentence or a blank page as a temporary wall, knowing it will come down, and probably in the next fifteen minutes.

That is an enormous difference.

Writing is thinking. The thinking is in the writing; it is not *about* the writing, and it doesn't come before it; the thinking lies in the process of writing. Trying to think outside of that process won't do you much good.

I believe I have finally discovered the answer to the eternal problem that students complain of when trying to write papers in English 101. (Not that the problem stops there; no, it continues on forever.) "I don't know what's wrong," a student says. "I've got these words in my head that I can't get down on paper." How familiar and how true. The same thing happens to me, but I write around what I want to say. The problem is that you can't really think out beforehand whatever it is you're going to say. The writing of it is the thinking of it. In other words, don't think, write. That sounds as if it's leaning lemminglike over the edge of impossibility, but it's true.

Drinking helped me with such mental acrobatics. If there's anything that releases you from forced thought, it's a stiff drink. Perhaps just as important, it's company, and company is one of the things that drinking is very much about.

On the other hand, on those occasions when I had a drink while writing, the writing came with a certain ease. (Was this the easeful thought I so wished for?) If that's the case, why not keep on drinking? There are many writers who would lay claim to alcohol helping their writing, giving it an edge.

So what was the problem?

I don't know the answer, aside from the enormous difference mentioned above. Perhaps it's that thought shouldn't be easeful; writing shouldn't be easeful; it shouldn't feel as if it's smooth and seamless.

That's not exactly the right answer, since writing does become easier, drinking or not, when you find you're in a groove. Or, as Stephen King wonderfully put it, when "you fall through a hole in the page."

You forget what you're doing and do it. What do you know? That sounds almost like drinking.

But drinking takes no effort. Writing takes an enormous amount, which is why more people don't do it.

We'd rather drink.

17

KG

"You'll Never Eat Lunch
in This Town Again"

I was sober for nine months and in recovery when I was twenty-six years old and working as a book publicist at Random House. During that time, I had the opportunity to spend a month with an author who changed my life and taught me some lessons about those who can't surrender to this disease. I kept a diary of the time I spent in New York City with her. Here is some of what we grappled with together and apart.

Julia Phillips—the producer of *Close Encounters of the Third Kind* and *The Sting* and *Taxi Driver* (all of them favorite films)—rolled into town to promote *You'll Never Eat Lunch in This Town Again*, an explosive tell-all about Hollywood in the 1970s and her personal destruction through booze and drugs.

Julia had it all. Funny, smart, and young. She was the first woman to win an Oscar as a producer—at age twenty-nine, for *The Sting*—and she went to the Academy Awards high on Valium, coke, and pot. Her acceptance speech brought down the house when she uttered the immortal "You don't know what a trip it is for a Jewish girl from Great Neck to meet Liz Taylor and win an Academy Award in the same night."

She went on to destroy her career over and over with freebase cocaine (a high so scary that even I wouldn't go near it) from 1978 to 1980. In those three years, she smoked and spent somewhere between seven to ten million dollars.

She kicked the cocaine habit, but she still liked her vodka and marijuana and smoked four packs a day, thank you very much. A rigorous workout regimen and a spiky hairdo kept her looking youthful. Energy came off of her in waves. Julia was the type of drunk who ran umpteen miles on the StairMaster in her suite at a ritzy hotel overlooking Central Park while watching TV and jabbering on the phone, smokes and bottle of vodka on the coffee table nearby.

A week before her book tour, she threatened to cancel all the interviews our publicity department had arranged, screaming at the director of publicity in Los Angeles, "I walked away from *Close Encounters of the Third Kind,* and I can walk away from this!"

That was just the beginning. Book tours are carefully constructed edifices built on staggered interviews, with each national media outlet demanding to be first, second, et cetera, in print, then broadcast, followed by appearances in major cities. Trying to recast the cement a week before the start of the tour would be murder, but I was told to do it. Hers was our biggest book of the spring season.

Julia soon proved to me that she had her finger on the pulse of popular culture. After her tirade, she told me in her gravelly voice,

"Ken, this book is going to number one on the *New York Times* best-seller list. I know what I'm doing."

So I tore up the schedule and planted an item in the *New York Post*'s influential "Page Six" column about the book and the commotion it was making in Los Angeles. I immediately received six phone calls from major television programs including an offer from *Donahue* to have Julia on for the whole hour, an honor usually bestowed only upon Hollywood actors.

This meant I had to cancel the guaranteed commitment with Joan Rivers, whom I personally had promised would get Julia first, before the book became a cause célèbre. The public relations business is a strange one: Rarely is anything put on paper. It's all handshake agreements built on trust, with a publicist knowing that if he pisses off a producer at a national TV show or a prominent magazine or newspaper, then not only will he be persona non grata, his whole company would take a black eye for all of the authors.

All of this was running through my head when I decided that, instead of having a driver and a limo pick up Julia, I would go along for the ride and be at JFK airport to greet her at midnight. I thought she would appreciate some groveling, Hollywood-style, to impress upon her how important her book was to the company.

It worked. She came down the runway, a thin, tiny woman with a sly smile and her trademark shock of gray hair standing on end like a porcupine. Behind her was her assistant, Susan, tall, Los Angeles–pretty in revealing clothes, with a big mop of unruly brown hair. After we retrieved multiple steamer trunks of luggage and stepped into the limo, Julia complained bitterly about not being allowed to smoke on the six-hour flight and immediately lit a cigarette.

Her nonstop kibitzing continued until she ground out the ciga-rette, reached into her coat, lit up what was left of a joint, and pronounced, "Tomorrow I start A.A.!"

We all laughed, particularly since I had told Susan I was in recov-ery, and we had one of those friendly, falsely intimate moments found only in the Los Angeles entertainment community. Susan was knowledgeable about the twelve steps, and we both couldn't help loving Julia. The sickly-sweet smell permeated the limo with Julia's every puff—the car windows up, of course—making my eyes water and my mouth dry.

To get in Julia's good graces, I fired off the unintentionally funny line (as only the young and ambitious can): "Julia, in my three and a half years of book publicity, I've never worked on a book this big!" Julia was thrilled. When we arrived at the Ritz-Carlton on Central Park, she and Susan went inside, and I got the bonus of a ride to my apartment in downtown Manhattan, filled with hope and foreboding.

Much to my surprise, *Donahue* went very well. Julia sold the book, was funny and honest, and handled all of Phil's questions with aplomb. She was on best behavior, and orders for the book soared.

After an action-packed day at work on Julia's and other books, I went to pick up "Jules" at ten P.M. for her eleven-to-midnight inter-view on *The Larry King Show*. This was before his show on CNN, when his radio show was a mainstay for big-name touring authors. I called up to the suite, and Susan warned me, "Be careful. She's really tired and in a bad mood."

I took the elevator up and entered the room, where Julia was sitting at a table with her best friend, the editor in chief of Ran-dom House. "Jules" was visibly pissed.

"Ken, you've made me do too much today. I'm tired, I haven't gotten enough sleep—don't you understand? I'm a forty-seven-year-old woman, and I can't take it." And on. And on. I stood there stone-faced, quickly factoring in the projected length of this tongue-lashing, the amount of time it would take to drive to Larry King's studio, the traffic in midtown this time of night, knowing that if I fucked up on getting her to the most important national live radio show in the country, it would be my head.

I finally got her out of the hotel and into the limo and she turned to me and apologized. "Ken, I'm sorry. I wouldn't normally do that in front of other people, but you have to understand, I'm really tired."

We arrived at the studio with eight minutes to spare before the show went live. Julia turned on the charm with Larry and killed the whole hour. I took her back to the hotel and dropped her off, desperately needing a twelve-step meeting.

As I attempted to go to sleep, I ran Julia's life through my head. I loved all that Julia had done because I was a movie buff. I couldn't possibly compare my talents to hers, but I did relate to how my choices had been dictated by alcohol and drugs.

I woke up the next day, exhausted. The strain of getting Julia to Larry King's show had worn me out. I slept late, and when I got to work, I discovered that Julia was refusing to do Howard Stern's radio show because she was too tired. Groaning, I picked up the phone and called Stern's infamous producer and on-air foil, Gary Dell'Abate, and told him that Julia was very tired, overworked, and couldn't come to the studio to do the show.

Gary screamed at me, "Phillips is sucking every dick in town but blowing off Howard? You gotta be fucking kidding me!"

Gary threatened that Howard would ridicule Julia on-air and

make her look really bad, and "this ain't an idle threat" (the following day, Howard did complain bitterly about Julia on-air). I apologized for fifteen minutes and then dragged myself into the weekly marketing-cum-torture meeting for the big-shot editors who ran Random House, a meeting reviled by everyone in our department; one of my friends threw up out of anxiety before going into the meeting. Many of the editors were nice, but the most self-important would sit imperiously and grill the unlucky PR people who had to describe the publicity gained—or lost—for the lead titles that week. Those oh-so-often-dog-shit titles for which they had overpaid, for which publicity was supposed to spin into gold.

This week was different. The publisher and the editor of Julia's book were very pleasant to me. In the meeting, my sterling imitation of Julia's gravelly exclamations had brought down the house. After the meeting, I told the editor—who was very cute—that I appreciated her being nice, and she replied, "You know, Ken, it's not like it's a hard thing to do." Yeah, right.

A few hours later, I was back outside our office building in midtown, waiting for a limo to take Julia and me to a popular live midday talk show on CNN. The limo was fifteen minutes late. I began to panic. Julia was waiting at the hotel. I saw a limo go by with a driver who looked like Julia's, and I ran two blocks, desperately trying to catch up. When I got to a red light where the limo had stopped and peered inside, it wasn't the same driver. I ran back to work—no cell phones in those days, so I had to go to my office to call the limo company. Apparently, the NYPD had chased the driver away, and he wound up in an auto accident. I told them to send a car to pick up Julia and decided it would be faster for me to run across town than take a car to the CNN studio.

Julia was fifteen minutes late and glowered at me as she stormed into the greenroom. I asked how she felt about just landing at number one on the *New York Times* best-seller list. She replied, "I'm really not surprised, I knew it all along," blah, blah, blah.

Julia went on the set, and was lit in to about some aspect of the book—Goldie Hawn's dirty hair?—while Susan and I caught up in the greenroom. Susan told me that Julia was always asking if she gossiped about how crazy her boss acted. I said Julia must be watching a movie of her own life: She could see her own awful behavior as if it were up on the screen, but she was unwilling, even powerless, to stop herself. Susan agreed. After the show, I dropped them both off at the hotel and went back to work, feeling so nauseated that I thought I was going to throw up.

The twelve-step slogan "Don't get too hungry, angry, lonely, or tired" reminded me I'm always near-suicidal or -homicidal if I'm hungry. I polished off a sandwich and felt better.

Being with Julia that week strengthened my resolve not to pick up a drink or a drug. Her chain-smoking even helped me quit smoking cigarettes. I finally kicked the habit five months after Julia's book tour was over, only to discover the truth behind what I heard my first year of sobriety: "You're not really emotionally sober until you quit smoking." Nothing can block feelings, enhance a lonely or sad moment, or kill an unwanted emotion better than a cigarette.

My last day with Julia was typical of our week together. I had to cancel yet another interview, this time with WABC Radio's *The Joy Behar Show.* The producer was completely pissed, if slightly mollified when I told him I had canceled Howard Stern and that Julia wasn't doing any local New York City radio. The producer went on to tell me that they'd advertised the interview twice in the papers and that, in canceling, "You're making us look like assholes."

I apologized profusely for another fifteen minutes (all of my apologies seemed to last that long), and the producer calmed down before hanging up on me.

I walked over to the hotel and picked up Julia for a taped NPR interview with *Weekend All Things Considered,* a top author-interview show. Julia was in a great mood, relieved that I wasn't wearing a suit on this Friday afternoon but had come in my "play clothes." She asked me, "Ken, tell me the truth, am I *the most* difficult author you've ever worked with?"

"No, I've worked with tougher." I mentioned an author we both knew, and we burst out laughing.

The interview was not one of the host's best; he stumbled and was off his game. After it was over, Julia complained, then invited me to her hotel for a drink, apparently unaware that I was sober. Though it seemed to be an olive branch for all of her antics, I politely declined. It was the last time I saw her.

Julia died twelve years later, in 2002, of cancer. She was fifty-seven.

I was sad the day I heard she died. I even forgave her for calling me "Random House PR boy" in her follow-up book, *Driving Under the Affluence.* Her charm, wit, and sixth sense for the marketing of culture made her much more than another Hollywood *Day of the Locusts*–type story.

For me, the experience of working on a number one *New York Times* best seller, of handling the world's most difficult person for a month, was an education. I honed my PR chops and saw up close how an incredibly intelligent, warm, and charming person could self-destruct because she couldn't stop drinking. Julia's excuse was "twelve-steps meetings are about religion, and I'm an atheist."

You'll Never Eat Lunch in This Town Again was a self-destructive act that got Julia Phillips—whom everyone in the entertainment industry had written off and forgotten—back on the front page of entertainment news. She had lunch in Los Angeles again. She got her second act, if not sobriety. I was nearly fired from my job just a few months earlier for having a difficult personality and being intolerant of my coworkers, but largely because of my work on this book, I was able to save my job. I earned a second act and sobriety by attending lunchtime twelve-step meetings to keep my sanity.

For all of her bravado and slams of the film industry, Julia had loved her work, every last minute of it.

Maybe, like Julia, I wanted to eat lunch in my town again.

18

MG

Downtime

I wonder sometimes why I bother. At times I feel almost as much a prisoner of sobriety as I did once of drunkenness. What's the point of this liquor-free life? Do I feel better? I don't know. Am I healthier? Probably. Do I look better? No. Am I easier to get along with? Yes, depending.

The clinic would call this kind of halfhearted attitude denial. Indeed, if the doctor read what I'm writing here, he'd want me back in the clinic tout de suite.

I think of the freedom of that woman my mother mentioned, the one who sat at her window every evening, reading and drinking two highballs. She had the freedom to do that. I don't.

I hear the friendly voices in the clinic telling me, Oh, but you *do* have that freedom! You're freer than she is. She has to have those drinks every evening. She's locked in to that particular prison. But you—you're out of it.

Why does that sound like a lie? If I'm out of that prison, I'm still on parole. "An alcoholic is never cured; he's always recovering." That's bad news right there. How much effort would you want to expend on solving a problem that you're told in the end cannot be solved? Am I supposed to be placated by the knowledge that I'm my own parole officer?

Here's the thing: It would be almost as hard for me now to have a drink as it was back then to refuse one. I'm locked in to my own stiff psychology. I seem to have exchanged one prison for another. (Or perhaps that's sophistry. Or denial.)

I haven't had a drink in two decades. No, it's even longer than that. I haven't pinned down my nondrinking history, as Ken has. He knows day-month-year. Do I consider it less important than he does? I must, and that could be a bad thing. I remember that I stopped two days short of the New Year. But which New Year?

I do remember my faux lapse on a flight when the attendant served me a martini by mistake. I'm set to wondering again: Why bother? Why not jettison this whole sober life? This brings me back to square one, after I've handed out a lot of reasons for not drinking. Good reasons abound: Do I show more self-restraint? Yes. Does food taste better? Of course not. Have I laughed as hard not drinking as I used to laugh with the same person after belting down a few? Yes, I think I have. Do I have as much fun at social functions? Absolutely not. To have fun at a social function, you've got to be drunk or eight years old.

To commemorate a member being sober for a month, a year, ten years, they are always handing out coins in A.A., the way my kindergarten teacher handed out paper hearts to those who had shown some hint of extra-goodness. I wonder if it has to do with our kindergarten selves, stripped of our adult allegiances to the trendy and the cool (like *Mad Men* without cigarettes), when drugs did not abound and escape meant not a substance but an open door.

Did it work?

I would have to ask, To do what?

You would say, To make you happy.

No. (Should it have?) Other things, like age, came along to knock the slats out from under that. I'm not sure, really, how *un*happy I was, drinking. The memory of an alcoholic isn't all that reliable.

Am I glad I stopped? Yes. I only wish the rewards were more obvious. For some people, the gains must be immense. If one can go from ruining one's prospects, one's family, one's work to reversing all of that, one wouldn't have to ask: Was it worth it? Did it work? It worked like a miracle.

I'm sure I felt a tremendous sense of relief not to be waging war on myself, not having to construct, every day, that architecture of the drinking life: whether to quit or carry on. Quitting put an end to the argument. The "why" fell by the wayside.

Twenty-odd years later, do I want to drink? Of course I do. When a truly exasperating day winds up, you bet I want to wind down over a cold martini. It's a desire as sharp as a knife of ice. If I were living with someone who drank, who rolled out the cocktail cart with the Absolut every evening, how would I resist? I think I would resist; I just wonder how.

If alcoholism is indeed a progressive disease (and I'm not at all sure it is), then I suppose I'd be drinking a lot more than I did, had I kept at it. I didn't drink until I passed out. I never passed out. Is that what I'd be doing? Somehow I doubt it.

It's always there, the possibility of drinking. That I could drink again and be none the worse. This is completely inconsistent with what I've said before, but none of this is ever settled, is it?

I have long since reached the age when friends are dead or gone. My best friend died years ago after many, many years of drinking. A doctor told her she would have to stop or die. She stopped. It was her heart that failed, but the irony is, I wonder if the abrupt cessation of the chief thing in her life killed her. It was a life she'd woven out of beer and cigarettes and martinis, and I imagine that, without it, her life unraveled as if it were a ghost life.

I was never particularly proud of myself for stopping. I think it was the drinking version of my mother's "anyone who can read, can cook."

My old friends Jim Beam and Gordon and Jack Daniel's. It would be nice to sit around a roaring fire and talk about the old days and relax, relax, relax, go down, go down, go down. Yes, it's always there, the possibility of that pale reunion, waiting for me to join it.

So why don't I? If I'm no longer persuaded by the best of arguments against drinking, why don't I?

The answer has to do with the failings of argument.

After all of the arguments have been settled, unsettled, resettled, I conclude that there is no argument. Nothing is settled; nothing ever was. Sober for twenty-two years does not mean sober for twenty-three. It does not mean the question is answered, the problem solved. Although twenty years would seem to be more proof of sobriety than twenty hours, I question that it would. I thought about drinking much more during my time in the Kolmac Clinic than I do now, but I don't believe I was closer to a drink.

I can hear my clinic colleagues argue, "Impossible! Of course you were closer to drinking then!" But that's argument, and argument can be unconvincing. Argument is faulty in any belief system—here, the belief being that alcoholic drinking is ruinous. You shouldn't drink.

If you try to argue your way out of a drink, you'll lose.

There comes a point when nothing can be depended upon; where the more you stand up in the boat to view that spit of land, the more dangerously the boat rocks.

T. S. Eliot says in "Little Gidding":

You are not here to verify,
Instruct yourself, or inform curiosity
Or carry report. You are here to kneel
Where prayer has been valid.

I don't know anything, I can't prove anything. There is evidence, yes, but the evidence is good only for that time and that place. It cannot be extrapolated and, like a downy blanket, thrown over every case, and every case proved to be the same case.

Me, I want some downtime.

That drinking is the only way (or any way) to get it is, of course, a lie.

Do I even know what downtime is? Or what it feels like?

It might be Eliot's "Zero summer." The paradoxical "Zero summer." That's a major contradiction in terms. Yet maybe that's the time and the place: the zero summer. The supposedly impossible.

Contradiction is what Kierkegaard came to; indeed, it was the only thing he depended upon: the belief in the absurd. The belief in what can never be known by means of argument, what he called the "leap of faith." He decided to believe in God because it was absurd to do so; there was no *reason* in the whole wide world for such belief. In a lesser way, it's like Edmund Hillary's mountain: There was no reason to climb it except it was there.

I'm not talking about God, faith, or prayer in any conventional sense. The mountain climb, the leap of faith. I don't belong to any church, not even the church of A.A. Or maybe I belong to this church, congregation of one.

Cheers.

19

MG

Alcohol, *C'est Moi*

I'm sitting in the tiny waiting area of a French restaurant. These few seats happen to be right next to the bar, where the bartender has set a martini (straight up, with a twist) before a woman smoking a cigarette and talking to her friend. The glass sits there. It's large, fan-shaped, fogged with ice; I can see the tiny rivulets running down the side like rain. She hasn't picked it up before we are shown to our table. For all I know, it might still be sitting there like a sign or a signal.

Waiting.

I identify completely with that drink on the bar.

Yet the advice I'm given in one how-to book after another talks as if it doesn't realize that I'm the drink on the bar.

The advice is always the same (and useless): During the time I would ordinarily be drinking, I should exercise, or read a book, or go to a movie, or cook a gourmet meal. And not hang out with my former drinking friends. I should reconnect with my nondrinking friends. How many friends do they think I have? They make it sound as if there's an army of them over the hill, just waiting to engage.

And be sure to avoid triggers, those things that really make an alcoholic want to drink. The assumption is that there are only certain times or objects or people that start you on your way to the drinks table. (The assumption also is that triggers always operate in the conscious mind.) The reason this bit of advice is vague is because anything can start an alcoholic on her way to the drinks table, or down to Swill's, or next door to see Lucy, who always has a cold bottle of Ultimat or Grey Goose chilling in the freezer. Anything can trigger it.

In other words, these how-to-stop-drinking books are telling me to get a(nother) life. All this advice can be distilled (not, unfortunately, like Absolut) to this: Find something to take the place of that drink you crave.

What? Are these books kidding? *Nothing* can take the place of that frosty martini on the bar; those shadowed glasses of Château Lafite on the table of that couple eating *boeuf*-something; that black Guinness foaming up beneath the bar pull until its creamy top is knifed smooth; that globe of Rémy warming in that gentleman's fingers. Nothing can take their place.

It's as if the consensus among those who treat or write about alcoholics is that we're dumb. In some way, this might be true; hence, A.A.'s dictum to "Keep It Simple." But I'm sick and tired of books that treat me like an idiot.

Read a book? Good. I'm choosing Fitzgerald's "The Crack-Up," or anything by Hemingway, so that I can at least enjoy a drink by proxy while being instructed on the fatal effects of drink.

Cook a gourmet meal? Now, tell me this: What alcoholic could bear to eat a gourmet meal without some of that Bordeaux gracing the table? A gourmet meal without wine? My God. The ocean without the shore.

Call these things distractions if you call them anything, but do not say they're taking the place of the cocktail hour or the session with the guys at Swill's.

C'est moi.

When Flaubert said this of Emma Bovary, he meant his identification with her was complete. It would seem to be his fate.

One is inclined to think the same thing of genetic makeup and, in our case, the determination of alcoholism, as in the studies of genes handed down from alcoholic parents to children.

With a gene, it isn't *c'est moi.* We seem to believe a gene shoots a behavioral characteristic arrow-straight. It doesn't. Genes are some distance back from any particular behavior, so genes are destiny only in the sense that character is destiny: There's a lot of room for modification. If parents are alcoholics, there is a predisposition toward the child's becoming one, but it's only a possibility—or, if one insists, a probability. It is by no means a certainty.

This *identification* with the object (in Flaubert's case, with Emma) might also be perfectly true of an alcoholic's identification with alcohol. It is so complete, it would seem to be one's fate. An alcoholic will drink no matter what; no, he has to drink no matter what. The choice has ceased to be rational. Therefore, what about appeals to rationality? Well, he doesn't give a toss for those. I shouldn't put it that way: He does give a toss, and he thinks someday he might be able to kick the habit. Just not today.

One appeals to his rational mind by observing, say, that he's making everyone around him miserable; or, say, that he's losing

job after job; or, say, that he seems to be making himself miserable. And on and on. There are more reasons (meaning reasonable,
meaning rational) for quitting than there are for continuing, and
probably every alcoholic knows that (at least the ones who admit
to the "disease").

What we have here is "alcohol, *c'est moi.*" Sorry, but that's the
way it is. I'm the drink, the drink is me. The pleasure/pain principle isn't working here. And one depends upon that principle to
get an alcoholic to see sense.

We are all after endorphins or, rather, the effects of endorphins,
our personal little supply of opiates, our morphinelike substances:
Runners, weight lifters, drinkers, gamblers are after endorphins,
the substance that carries us along on a euphoric wave, a rush.

There is a drug called naltrexone that blocks the effects of
endorphins. One has to take it while drinking! Can't you hear the
howls? A drug that encourages the alcoholic to drink? Not Anta-
buse, the one that makes you sick if you drink. No, that drug does
nothing at all if you don't drink while you're taking it. The point
is that alcohol releases endorphins into the brain, and naltrexone
blocks the effects. No rush, no euphoria. No rush? Why drink?

An alcoholic would undoubtedly agree. Except he'd turn it on
its head.

No rush? No, thanks. You take that stuff.

Me, I'll take this drink at my elbow.

C'est moi.

20

Sober Hotel

The beautiful girl with the cracked green and blue eyes turned to me in front of the refrigerator and said, "It's hard getting sober when you're young." I instantly knew what she meant, in that way people in recovery can communicate in shorthand. I was twenty-five and had no career, no marriage, no kids, nothing to give me any shape or dimension. Nick Hornby in his novel *High Fidelity* wrote, "It's not what you're like, it's what you like." I defined myself by my likes in music, sports, and some politics. Other than connecting those few dots, that was it when it came to understanding myself. Alcohol and drugs had caused me to truly lead the unexamined life.

I turned from the girl and looked at some other young people around the kitchen table. When my sponsor, Carl, invited me to his sober beach house in the Hamptons during my first month of sobriety, I said yes. Carl and his friend John talked about people in the house, bike riding, twelve-step meetings as we sped across Long Island. I fidgeted and looked out the window.

These two guys were best friends—tall, athletic, younger than I was, and more popular with girls than I would ever be. I wondered what I was doing there and how I would get through a weekend of not drinking at the beach with a houseful of strangers.

Occasionally, they'd turn and ask a question about my status as an alcoholic:

"What! You have a job? No way."

"What? And you have a driver's license? Dude, are you sure you're an alcoholic?"

I had done a Hamptons share house during my first summer in New York City, and it was a disaster. All of the girls were big-game hunters, looking for Wall Street guys with slicked-back hair and money to burn at nightclubs and expensive restaurants. With my pathetic wardrobe and eighteen-grand-a-year salary, I was getting nothing and not liking it. The bar scene was a nightmare and everything horrendously overpriced. I never wanted to go back.

When Carl, John, and I finally stopped for gas, I went into the convenience store, bought a pack of cigarettes, and looked longingly at the six-packs behind the walk-in glass doors. Bud, Bud Light, Michelob, Coors, all of my best friends sitting side by side, twinkling in the artificial light.

"I'm going to get a six-pack," I said to myself. "Fuck them and not drinking." The sensation passed. I paid for the cigarettes and got in the car and grunted when my sponsor asked me how I was doing.

We pulled up in front of a mansion from the days of Gatsby, a massive house with faded, chipped white paint and a big front porch. Young men and woman lounged outside and yelled greetings to my sponsor and his friend. As I got out of the car, I was dying for a can of beer to take the edge off, and to give me something to hold, something to do.

I was under the assumption (which could be the title of another book) that when I arrived at the beach house, my sponsor and his friend would walk me around the whole weekend introducing me to everyone, taking me to meetings, and basically making sure I was happy and feeling good twenty-four hours a day. I was wrong.

After we dropped our luggage on the floor of the large, sun-dappled room with six single beds, they both disappeared. I hardly saw them again for the rest of the weekend. I was left to drift around the huge house, up and down the massive oak stairs, bumping into people who were talking earnestly about recovery. Peals of laughter could be heard from the porch as drunken war stories were retold. I was full of fear and false bravado, but what made me anxious was the fear of not being able to sleep. I'd had a problem sleeping since I was a kid, terrified of the nightmares I had practically every night.

One of the two founders of the sober beach house was a very kind "older" man (by that I mean late forties, positively ancient to me at the time), and I asked him if I could sleep on the couch in the living room. He smiled kindly and said it would be breaking a rule, but sure, I could sleep downstairs if I needed to. That was a relief.

Saturday afternoon I couldn't wait to get the hell to the beach, where I could separate myself from everyone and jump into the ocean. My sponsor loaded me into his car with a few other guys, and I brought my Frisbee so I could do at least one thing I was good at—spinning my Frisbee on my finger and doing spins, back rolls, and other tricks I had spent countless hours practicing in high school.

I trudged down to the famed white-sand beach, threw down my towel, and ran into the water. It was freezing but felt good. I swam for a while, staring at the cluster of sober people on the beach, laughing and talking, with no alcohol in sight. I just couldn't understand it.

I emerged from the ocean and asked my sponsor if he'd throw the Frisbee with me. A real jock, he jumped up, and we began to toss it back and forth. At last I was on my turf; he might play a killer game of tennis (a country-club sport I barely understood, rivaled only by my lack of knowledge about—and interest in— golf), lift some mean weights, and know every girl in the beach house, but I was confident I was the only one who could deliver an expert forehand toss twenty yards down the beach or spin a Frisbee behind my back.

After five minutes, I was trying a particularly difficult one-handed catch behind my back when I heard my swimsuit rip. I had torn the rear of the suit in half. In a panic, I waved to my sponsor and yelled something about needing to rest and ran to my towel, where I sat for the next two hours without moving. I was totally embarrassed and feared I would be laughed at. I would rather die than be laughed at.

I sat watching the ocean, not talking to anyone, reading. Other than Frisbee and rock music, reading was my only passion. I didn't want to be alone, but I was completely tongue-tied. I had a split swimsuit and no beer to drink, so I burrowed into the sand and read. This sucked. It was shaping up to be the worst weekend of my life. If this was what being sober was all about, I had no idea how I was going to do it. Oh, sure, "One day at a time." We all knew that meant: "Never drink again. Period."

Every night the beach house had twelve-step meetings where, as a newcomer, I was encouraged to speak up. I can't remember what I muttered when it was my turn. That Saturday was nothing more than the meeting, dinner, people talking, and then time to go to bed. John had a girlfriend he wanted to see, and my sponsor disappeared again. I had to go to sleep, mind racing, no beer, in a strange place, in a room with five other beds, all occupied by alcoholics. I had decided to be brave and sleep upstairs. Now I regretted it. As an only child used to having my own room, I was petrified. I lay there trying to go to sleep. After an hour, I finally seemed to be dozing, listening to the deep breathing and snores around me.

Suddenly, I heard John and his girlfriend giggling as they snuck into the room. I pretended to be sleeping as they crawled into the bed next to me, a few feet away.

Okay, they're just going to crash here, nothing to worry about, I thought.

A few minutes later, the bed started creaking, and their moans became audible. Oh. No.

I didn't know what to do. This didn't seem very sober, whatever "sober" meant. I couldn't lie there for the next twenty minutes and listen to them while the rest of the guys slept, but to get up and let them know I'd been listening would be horribly embarrassing for me (and, I assumed, for them).

I couldn't take it anymore. In one swift move, I got up with the top sheet wrapped around my shoulders and left the room. Quietly, I padded down the stairs and headed for the porch, thinking that would be a quiet spot to sit and rest and chain-smoke. To my surprise, there were three other guys on the porch, even though it was well past midnight. Apparently, they were newcomers who couldn't sleep, either. One of them was chewing tobacco and introduced himself. "I'm Dayton. I've got a hundred and six days, want some chew?" I immediately said yes and dipped into the Copenhagen, my first drug of choice when I was twelve. I started talking to him while spitting off the porch onto the grass. I was envious that he had fifty-six days more sobriety than I did and had already crossed the magic ninety-day mark.

He was funny, and most important, he was a huge fan of the Grateful Dead, my favorite band and the shaky cornerstone that much of my self-image had been founded on. As we talked through the night, I reached a degree of comfort and eventually grew tired enough to go back upstairs, fling myself into bed, ignore the couple next to me in their postcoital slumber, and sleep.

Although I hated most of the weekend, found the drive back to the city long and boring, and could never imagine doing it again, something stuck. I had a real-life model of people of all ages— particularly young people—laughing and seeming to genuinely like and care for one another, who could talk about how crazy they were with no fear of repudiation.

Much to my surprise, after ten months of trying to do it mostly alone, taking a series of girlfriends "hostage" as a panacea for all the emotions beginning to bubble up, I found myself at an office in midtown Manhattan in May, signing up for the summer sober beach house. There I was, laughing with Dayton and a couple of other guys I had met in meetings and liked, signing on the dotted line. And I had the money to pay for it.

Just as my mother's hotel became the furnace that forged her life and her world view, my sober beach house was responsible for the woman I married and six of my groomsmen. The men I met in the program became the best friends I could ever hope for, the sober house the beginning of a process of redemption that I could never imagine while sitting on the beach in a ripped swimsuit.

SECOND CONVERSATION:
DENIAL AND POWERLESSNESS

MG: Denial is the biggest danger in addiction. Denial is a concept I have always found fascinating, since the person who's using it really doesn't think he's denying. Those of us who aren't addicts simply don't believe it's possible: The subject being denied is so obvious that the person denying it must be aware of it. (Here again is a thumbs-down to anyone who believes that people act rationally.)

Denial so easily leads to the beginning of something prefaced by "Just one drink wouldn't hurt." Now, the whole machinery of alcoholism is built on this theory: It's *never* just one drink. Never. If you can do just one drink and feel relatively satisfied, then you're not an alcoholic. Drinkers who go back to drinking almost always begin by floating the just-one-drink argument.

The second biggest problem is bringing reason into the issue of addiction. If you can't bring reason to bear, the only other way to get sober is an intervention, but even that is bringing reason to bear in a way: "Can't you see what you're doing to me? Why can't you stop? All of us are saying you have a problem!" That's emotional, but at the same time, there's logic: If the drunk can see what he's doing to his family, then of course he'll stop.

The only thing that works is to toss an alcoholic in the car or on a plane and force him to go to rehab. Even then the denial keeps working, because most people don't get sober the first time they go. Since you [Ken] didn't go

143

to rehab, I assume you weren't in as bad shape, so there must not have been as much denial.

KG: What are you talking about? I was in denial from the first time I started partying with my friends in high school, because I didn't want to drink or smoke pot, but I did it to fit in.

MG: Denial is more complicated. It's elusive, paradoxical, even magical. It's the rabbit out of the hat; it's the unending line of colored scarves pulled from the pocket; it's the lady sawed in half.

Denial is the art of saying you're not doing something even as you're doing it, which is more complex than simply saying, "No, this drinking, this drugging, isn't affecting my life," while your life lies in tatters around you.

KG: I disagree. You can be self-aware and in denial at the same time. In my version, I can have enough self-awareness to know that going on a forty-eight-hour bender was bad for me, but I did it anyway, because I wanted to have fun and didn't give a damn about the consequences.

I'd say, "I can get away with this, it doesn't matter, no one will know, I'm still getting good grades," even though the evidence showed it *did* matter—conflicts with you, grades not as good as they could have been, taking the SATs completely hungover, hanging out with lowlifes up in western Maryland or Washington, D.C., or in England. I knew that consuming these chemicals was making my life worse, but I didn't want to stop. It was even worse in college, and I knew it, but I refused to do anything about it, because I denied it.

MG: That's not denial; it's refusal. Refusal is much more straightforward. Denial is the art of hiding from yourself. You're not wholly knowable to yourself.

KG: Well . . . perhaps. One of the worst cases of denial I've ever seen was that of a friend of mine who had a terrible drinking problem but refused to admit it, or pretended he couldn't see it. Wait: Perhaps I shouldn't say "refused" and "pretended." That's probably the point: He *didn't* see the problem, or at least not the extent of the problem.

As I was staring at him one day, I could see something flickering behind his eyes, a truth that wanted to get out, a desire to admit he couldn't stop—but it disappeared, and I've never talked to him about it again. I could see the denial warring with the truth, and the truth lost.

MG: Now, *that* is *denial,* a superb example.

KG: The literature of recovery states that "understanding and insight were not enough." Bill Wilson—the founder of A.A.—*knew* he shouldn't drink again after the scores of times he sobered up only to get drunk again. He was on this horrible downward spiral for years because he crazily thought he could still have a drink, one or two, and then stop. I can have that first drink, is what he thought.

According to Bill, the number one obsession for an alcoholic is that he can drink like a normal person.

MG: Yes, it's a kind of magical thinking: I do it, but I don't do it to the extent they think I do it. But it sounds as if you knew it while it was all going on.

KG: Yes, I did, but I denied it [laughs].

MG: I still say that's not denial. You knew but you refused to stop because you were addicted. It doesn't sound as if you were completely in the dark in the beginning. At the end, perhaps you were.

What accompanies this is the denial of the people around the drunk—the wife, parents, children, friends, they all try and deny it as long as possible because they can't stand the idea of the person they love being a drunk. You said that in Al-Anon, people affected by an alcoholic have as much of a problem as the alcoholics, which is, I think, devastating news. And it gets at the extreme complexity of alcoholism.

I know you believe in the "disease" model of alcoholism and addiction. Say for the moment that it's more of a learned behavior. Let's say, for example, that Joe's social drinking turns into alcoholic drinking. Joe's wife, Betty—with whom he has a rocky relationship anyway—sees this but tries to deny it because she doesn't want to be married to a drunk. Actually, she doesn't want to be married to Joe very much, and the alcoholism—which she can no longer ignore, not with Joe lying on the kitchen floor every night—becomes a weapon. Under the pretense of wanting him to stop drinking, she keeps berating him, which makes him drink more. The drinking becomes something like a Ping-Pong ball they shove back and forth across the table, neither one willing to put down the paddle. Because they both want to win the game. I'd bet that's what's going on in the minds of a lot of people in Al-Anon, all while they're acting like victims. What they (we) want is to play the game and win. And if Joe sobers up, uh-oh! There goes the game.

KG: Absolutely! In fact, some would argue that the Al-Anonic's behavior gets even crazier than the drunk's.

MG: So we're doubling the problem. It leads us back to reason: why people struggle with bringing reason to a problem that is not conducive to reason. You cannot reason a problem out of existence when the problem resists reason at every single turn. The irony is that the only thing any of us has to use in dealing with problems is reason, or logic.

Here is someone who appears to be ruining his own life and the lives of other people. What can we use except reason and logic? But that's not going to get you very far. So what are you going to do? What's the answer?

KG: There is no answer. Which is not what Americans want to hear: We're a results-oriented country, not as interested in moral shades of gray, say, as are the French or Germans. Twelve-step programs were founded by two Americans. The steps are very action-oriented and try to solve an unsolvable riddle. What describes America better than that?

The American psyche says, "If there's a road that ends, knock down the wall or plow a new road." The fact of the matter is that twelve-step programs have a far better record of helping people with alcoholism, gambling, overeating, sex addictions, overspending, you name it. In the end, the success rate is never going to get to 50 percent, 60 percent, 70 percent, because of the riddle we just described, a problem that defies logic and rationality.

MG: I've come to the conclusion that the really big block when it comes to twelve-step programs is the insistence on powerlessness. Why some alcoholics prefer Rational Recovery and Moderation Management is that these organizations are completely, adamantly against the idea of powerlessness.

Both organizations look at excessive drinking entirely from the position of self-reliance. We know there's some success, because they let people keep on drinking. Still, all of these groups appear to be dead set against the idea of powerlessness, which means turning one's life over to a Higher Power. Most people equate "Higher Power" with God, despite the insistence that a Higher Power can be anything at all that one conceives of as transcending self. I wonder, though, if the notion of the Higher Power is how twelve-step programs really indoctrinate people. Isn't the so-called Higher Power God in disguise?

KG: In essence, yes.

MG: Exactly! There is a religious—or, if you prefer, spiritual—underpinning to the whole organization, which is not at all a criticism, just an observation. Now, here's the thing. A group like Moderation Management says that you can drink in moderation and learn how to drink safely if you work at it and schedule it properly. In other words, you can control your drinking. I wouldn't say this is total nonsense, for I imagine that some people in this group—or out of it—do manage to control their drinking. But I also think they spend a lot of time thinking about drinking, and that, to me, would sap a lot of pleasure from drinking. So there's no Higher Power to appeal to, to keep you off the bottle; you've got to keep track of your drinks. "Now, how many more drinks can I have at this party?"

KG: Charting—

MG: Yes, keeping count. The question also lies in the word "problem" in the phrase "problem drinker." Some people look at having a problem with drinking as completely different from having an addiction. As far as I'm concerned, if you have a problem—

KG: A problem with drinking suggests that it's something the drinker can "solve."

MG: Right. Again, if you have to moderate your drinking, then it's *automatically* beyond being a problem. People who don't have a problem with drinking don't have to work to moderate their drinking; they just curtail it or cut it out altogether, as if they have a food allergy.

I'm a big believer in self-transcendence. I think everyone, at some time, for brief moments, attains self-transcendence. I remember once, driving in downtown D.C., I saw a row of ducklings crossing F Street. Traffic stopped, pedestrians stopped, everyone stopped to make sure those ducklings made it to the other side. And I bet everyone had a moment of transcendence when those ducklings were more important than their daily cares and worries. Everyone has moments—

KG: Uh-huh. Where nirvana is within reach.

MG: In drinking, that's what people are after.

KG: Carl Jung stated that alcoholics are engaged in a low-level search for spirituality.

MG: I wouldn't disagree with that at all.

KG: One way of looking at it is that alcoholics are seekers. Seeking something beyond the satisfactions of daily living. They want to dream greater dreams, climb greater heights . . .

MG: Come on, now. Don't you think this is true of most people? I'd be surprised if I found anyone who didn't want something beyond the material world—and its goods.

KG: Yeah, I agree, but the difference is, nonalcoholics don't look to get their freak on just because they had a bad day at the office. They come home, yell at their wives or kick their dog, turn on the TV, and tune out.

That's not enough for guys like me.

We're out for revenge. And revenge means oblivion, oblivion for ourselves, and oblivious to everyone else.

21

MG

Memory

I was twenty-four or twenty-five and working for the government in order to pull together enough money for graduate school. I took a night course at American University from a professor who was brilliant, intimidating, and enthralling. The subject was American literature, though I'm not certain of that; I seem to remember Emma Bovary creeping into a lecture. I have a recollection of one or more novels by Henry James. I do remember Jake Barnes in *The Sun Also Rises*. And Robert Penn Warren's *All the King's Men*.

This class was three hours long. Professor von Abele talked for the entire three hours. I cannot recall his ever referring to a note either in his hand or on the lectern. It was all in his head. Nor was it a class in which discussion was encouraged. Once in a great while, one of us (not I) would ask a question rather timidly. It would be answered and the lecture resumed. I got the impression that Dr. von Abele had so much to say that he didn't want to waste time answering questions.

Three hours, no notes, no breaks. Three straight hours, and that didn't seem to faze him. My mind skims over the course, recalling some of it, but mostly him and his presentation.

I do remember being impressed by something in a poem of Robert Penn Warren's. Not the whole poem, not much of it, except one line. The poem was "Original Sin," something about Harvard Yard. I have a clear remembrance of one metaphor. Not the subject of the metaphor, only the comparison, the "like" part. This was: "Like a mother who rises at night to seek a childhood picture."

That line has remained printed on my mind for half a century. Strange, but I have never gone back to the poem to see what the other half of the metaphor was. I don't know why. Back then I reacted oddly to it. Why would a mother do that? Why on earth would anyone get out of bed to go and find a childhood picture? Rather than just kick the line aside, indifferently, I felt hostile. It irritated me that I couldn't understand the action. I read the poem several times for the class, and each time I'd stumble over that line as if it were a barrier to something, a tree across my path. There was a gap between me and it that I didn't understand, and it made me unreasonably angry.

It's been a long time since I took that course and read that poem. It seems impossible that I can think of my life in that long season. A few years later, I was in Iowa City, teaching at the university and winding up in the writers' workshop and writing poetry. Ten years later, I got married. It was a disastrous marriage, not just because my husband and I were both alcoholics but because we were supremely unsuited. We acted like kids and argued and drank.

151

I knew before, during, and after that this marriage was a mistake of monumental proportions, and yet I did nothing to stop it or end it for years. Five years elapsed before I left. (Today, alas, five years were more like five days. Then, five years were more like fifty.) There must be a psychological equivalent of locked-in syndrome wherein you know, see, and hear everything that's going on; you just can't bring yourself to do anything about it. Or perhaps that is another example of denial.

That's a short voyage 'round my marriage. Except for its conversational excellence (we were both good talkers), it was not all that interesting, but it was embalmed for the ages.

Tolstoy's paradigm of family disposition—that all unhappy families are unhappy in their own way—I very much doubt. If you lined up ten teenagers and asked why they were unhappy with their parents, do you really think one of them *wouldn't* say, "I can't talk to them"? (Not that we're done with Tolstoy—has anyone ever been done with him?—for he was probably talking about the truths behind unhappiness; I'm talking only about our vacuous understanding of it.) I think all marriages are unhappy in the way of all others. There are bigger helpings of unhappiness on the plate, but it's still the same food.

So a child named Ken was born into this one. Fortunately, the baby was made to share this cauldron of eye of newt and tail of toad only for a little while, and he threw it on the floor anyway. Perhaps babies soak up unhappiness like sponges; if so, this baby squeezed it out again in smiles. I know it sounds like window dressing and overly fond recollection, but I swear he never woke me with crying; he was always smiling in the morning. You could put him anywhere—in a crib, in a playpen, in a closet (no, I didn't)—and he was happy.

There was something about him. He was neither grasping nor greedy. It always surprised me that we could go into the local Toys "R" Us in search of a present for a friend's birthday party, and Ken would help pick it out yet never ask for anything for himself. Where did he learn this graceful attitude with parents who were neither generous nor graceful?

I remember many library trips and many books, from *Gone Is Gone* and *The Wind in the Willows* to Edward Gorey and the dreadful fates that overtook the Gashleycrumb Tinies. Ken loved that book and would insist that his grandmother read it to him. She thought it entirely too macabre for a child: "'B is for Basil, assaulted by bears.' How dreadful!" "There's Neville," I argued. "'N is for Neville, who died of ennui.' That's not so bad." My mother had come to stay with us for a little while to help take care of Ken while I worked.

We lived in a trailer then, in Morgantown, West Virginia. That trailer. It was old, with two small bedrooms, a kitchen, a bath, and a little living room. I rented it from a nice couple who lived across the road. It had a porch where Ken liked to sit. I have a snapshot of him sitting with a big rabbit, a huge inflated thing that rose way above him.

I worked as a secretary for a man who did some sort of consulting for the University of West Virginia. He informed me one day when the paychecks rolled in that his withholding tax was more than my salary. I thanked him for sharing.

We were poor. I can't remember if there was money for vodka or wine. I doubt it, yet I can't imagine I wasn't drinking then, having drunk my way through five years of marriage. Since I'd gotten out of the marriage, though, it's possible that I didn't need to be propping myself up so much with alcohol.

Where we lived, there were few houses, so I don't know where the children came from that Halloween. Ken loved the trick-or-treaters. Halloween is his birthday, and he thought they had all dressed up just for him. I didn't tell him otherwise. It was pretty wonderful.

I'm thinking of a poem I wrote back in the poetry days of Iowa City called "Haunted Autumn," about a lot of little kids who go trick-or-treating. They tell the adults they know about a dark house with ghosts and witches, and they're going there to disappear. Then the poem gets larded up with growing up but not getting any wiser. It was published, but it wasn't very good, except for the kids who were going to that house to disappear.

I don't understand some of my poetry. There are a lot of houses in my poems: I'm obsessed with houses. There are a lot of children: I'm obsessed with children. "In a dark wood, the dark leaves fall / Around the darkest house of all." Apparently that is where the children are, but it also says that is where they want to be. "Only children / Carry within them the dead weight of houses." That was another poem about children and houses; if I understood that poem, I think I would understand a lot.

We left the trailer and went back to Washington. Then came the apartment in Silver Spring, the little house in Greenbelt, the larger house in Takoma Park. And the years of the Washington Waldorf School, that divine adjunct to childhood on the grounds of the Washington National Cathedral. I remember so well the headmaster, Dr. Kaufmann. If ever a person was born to teach, it had to be him. (I'll bet he had firsthand acquaintance with ghosts and witches and dark houses.)

I'm glossing over the surrealism of adolescence. What I want to know is, what happened? What happened to the little boy of two or three, that he came to feel life was so uncertain and chancy, so dangerous, that he had to go looking for safety in booze? It must have been a lack, a lack of love, support, something. Did he fear he was falling and looked for a safety net?

The story of parents and children is one of tragic implications. Its success depends on separation. It's as if, between the shutting and opening of a door, or turning away and turning back, everything changes. You wonder about a child: Where did you go?

What happened in these forty-odd years that wrought such volcanic changes? I don't think it was pot and beer and gin, or not wholly. It's something else, an inevitable downward spiral. The trouble is, we can't keep our hands on anything; things change at the slightest touch, even wood, even stone. We can't hold on to anything; it's like running our hands through water.

Yet there must be something. I wonder if Proust was right. I wonder if it's memory.

Sometimes I think there's a CEO somewhere in his office, successful and rich, kids grown up. His son is a surgeon, so much in demand that they barely have occasions to talk; his daughter is a painter of strange and unpredictable forms. His wife is still looking good because she can afford to. Trips to Europe, a ski chalet in the Swiss Alps; a summer house on Mount Desert Island. Dinner tonight with friends at the Four Seasons.

This CEO sits after all the other working stiffs have gone, sits in the dim nickel-plated light in his office overlooking Central Park, or Boston Common, or the Golden Gate Bridge. He's thinking about a trailer. He'd like to go back to it.

A sentimental fantasy. A cliché. But I have to tell myself stories.

I get up from my desk and walk aimlessly in air that looks almost dusty with the light of early October. I am no longer poor. Where I live now is a far cry from that trailer in Morgantown. Only it did have a porch, and I don't have one here. And Ken sat on the porch with a big rabbit. And the trick-or-treaters came.

It's nearly Halloween now.

I walk aimlessly, picking things up, putting them down, a small brass elephant, an ornament, a book . . .

Like a mother who rises at night to seek a childhood picture.

22

MG
———

A Lamp and a Menu

I'm sitting in a cabin in the woods outside of Frostburg, Maryland, thinking about dinner at the lodge. A menu has been left in the cabin, and the food, I understand, is very good, haute cuisine, indeed, which one wouldn't expect in the woods.

It's seven P.M., and at this time back in the day (as they say), I'd be working on my third martini (and that's a conservative guess). Instead, I'm only thinking of a martini. What I notice most in my mind's eye is the mist clinging to the glass like a rained-on window in which you might trace a heart.

If I could manage to get this description precise enough, if I could cut with a scalpel's precision, I swear I could drink the words straight up.

But I'm not drinking. Right now I'm thinking of stealing that lamp on the table over there. It's quite remarkable. The base is a wooden fish leaping from carved water. I thought the shade was marbled gold until I turned on the light and the whole panoramic fish scene sprang to life in silhouette. There is one fisherman with a net and another, farther around the shade, in a boat. Amid black pines, fish jump from painted water, black ducks move on the horizon, pigeons nosedive from the sepia sky or, as the incomparable Wallace Stevens put it, sink "downward to darkness, on extended wings."

If I could write a line like that, I would never, ever need to think about, much less drink, a martini.

They were both fishermen, my father and my brother, my father dead long ago, my brother a few years, though now that seems long ago, too. Time has a way of thinning out, like water over rocks.

My father had a cabin in the woods on an island in the Georgian Bay, the cabin reachable only by water. Although I wasn't there when my father was alive, I did go there when my brother was. It would be hard to beat that scene: sitting around a fireplace, talking and drinking before a supper of freshly caught trout and fried onions and potatoes. The air was so clear, it had a weight to it. There are fishermen who go up there alone. For some, isolation is a thing they can drink in.

I'm told that fishing requires patience. But everything requires patience—writing requires patience, standing in line at the supermarket requires it, waiting for the coffeemaker requires it. If we had the patience required of us, we'd be halfway to a peaceful life. Drinking, at least until the arc moves downward, gives the illusion of peace.

This cabin I occupy for a few days has a porch where I sit, rocking and looking up at the windswept treetops, congratulating myself on getting up out of the heat of D.C. on a whim (since

I usually have to plan out a trip to CVS before I make it), patting myself on the back for leaving behind computers and television. I have a cell phone that I don't use often; I don't like e-mail, so I don't check it often. Basically, I live offline, but I look for distractions just like anybody.

I've never been to the MacDowell Colony or Yaddo, those writers' colonies that have proved a godsend for writers and artists who couldn't otherwise find the time or place to work. Your breakfast and lunch are delivered, and except for joining your fellow writers and artists for dinner, you are left on your own.

Here, at this lodge, the same thing: They bring your breakfast in a box and place it on the porch. They do lunch this way, too, if asked. Dinner has one going to the lodge a quarter mile or so down the dirt road. We could be a bunch of writers and artists gathering for a social evening and a meal after a day of isolation.

When I'm at home, rarely does an entire uninterrupted day happen. All writers, if asked, would claim this is what they long for. Me, I don't know. I have a suspicion I would be a total failure at living for a month or six weeks at a writers' colony (where some writers stay, I think, as long as six months). I think to be successful in such a place must require a rigorous exercise of will.

I like to think I want only uninterrupted pieces of time to write; after all, I define myself that way—writing. Then again, I could be a fraud. Maybe I don't want that at all. Maybe I just want to shuffle ahead in bits and pieces, writing for a few minutes or hours. A blank page of time affects me, well, like a blank page. A threat. Do you think you can fill me up? it says. You?

The threat was much worse when I was drinking. I kept stumbling over writer's block. The inability to write for, say, fifteen whole minutes convinced me that I was washed up. I had absolutely no faith in my ability to pick myself up and go on.

The cabin-in-the-woods illusion goes skipping right along with the cottage by the sea, or the small house "of clay and wattles made." Such domains are for those souls who are just this side of living in hermitages and who don't need a Barnes & Noble on one side and a coffee shop on the other. I have always kidded myself about the cabin in the woods, when I wasn't looking at real estate photos in *Country Life* of ruined castle keeps in Scotland. Like the good little writer I am, I see myself in a house overlooking miles of wheat fields, or in a bayou with the alligators breaking the surface, and me, writing, writing, writing uninterruptedly all day long. The stuff of nightmares.

So I sit on the porch rocking, and looking at the treetops, and getting bored, and siding with Woody Allen: "Nature and I are two."

Inside, I'm stranded between a menu and a lamp. I'm thinking that this food deserves wine. Actually, I deserve wine, but I'll hold the food responsible.

A glass of wine. I stopped going to the clinic the first time after several months because I disliked my recovery group and its self-satisfied air. Within a couple of weeks of leaving, I had a glass of wine. I drank wine for a while, a few weeks or perhaps months, then, eventually and predictably, started in on the martinis again.

I get up to turn the lamp off and on again, so the dark images appear as if by magic. The fish leap out of parchment water; the fishermen cast their lines.

I wish they'd come back, my father and my brother, with their rods and reels.

I'm either going to have a glass of wine or steal that lamp.

Hello, my name is Martha, and I'm an alcoholic. Or a thief.

23

KG

Anger Management

One of the first things I heard when I got sober that I didn't understand until later was "Alcoholics are people whose lives get worse after they stop drinking."

In my third week of sobriety, my neck suddenly froze. I couldn't turn it to the left or right. I panicked and told a coworker that I was in pain. She directed me to Dr. John Sarno, an MD at New York University who had developed a theory and treatment for neck and back pain named tension myositis syndrome.

I called his office, and instead of a bored receptionist, a nurse asked how I felt. I told her I had stopped drinking and my neck was frozen, and she got me in to see Dr. Sarno the next day.

Dr. Sarno evaluated me through an extensive question-and-answer session, looked at my neck, and told me that he thought I had TMS. He explained that it was caused by suppressed emotions, the principal emotion being anger. He had me complete some written exercises and read his book. Within ten days, my neck was fine.

The following summer, after a year of sobriety, I quit smoking, only to be greeted by an explosion of anger. I had no idea how smoking cigarettes had masked my emotions. Even without alcohol and pot, as long as I could smoke those Marlboro Lights, I was okay. The minute I began to feel sad or frustrated or off-kilter, lighting up a cigarette made it all float away in a puff of smoke.

One day I wandered back to my office with a guy from my lunchtime twelve-step meeting. We talked about the first year. I said, "Man, I really didn't think I could do it. I didn't think I would make it. It was so hard."

He stopped, looked at me, and said, "Yeah, that first year was hard, but I'm warning you, the second year is much harder."

I wanted to kill him. Thanks for letting me enjoy my sobriety "anniversary." That was on top of the two-page hate letter that had just arrived at my office from a woman I had recently broken up with. She had five years of sobriety and was technically breaking the rules by dating someone with under a year, but she forgot that in her vitriol.

A month later, on one of the hottest days of the summer, I was walking down my block in Chelsea. I stopped to look at the broken glass on my street from a smashed car window, and I opened up a pack of cigarettes. I had tried to quit smoking numerous times when I was drinking, but I couldn't do it. I hadn't tried yet in sobriety; I had been too frightened to quit drinking *and* smoking at the same time.

I started to light up and felt an immediate revulsion. It was so hot, I didn't want to smoke. But I had the urge. It reminded me of drinking: not wanting to but having to. I threw the pack in the trash, and I haven't smoked a cigarette in twenty-one years. I had a flirtation with cigars in the mid-nineties when they were trendy, but I had to stop smoking them, too, because they made me sick to my stomach. Not that I didn't keep trying, even after they made me feel terrible.

I detoxified from cigarettes by returning to chewing tobacco. I would chew at Random House, spitting tobacco juice in an empty Pepsi can while Pulitzer Prize–winning authors were wandering the halls.

The chewing tobacco helped quell my physical urge to smoke but not the anger and frustration I felt more and more often. It blew straight out of me like a volcano. I broke two phones in my office by slamming down the receiver so hard, the plastic cracked. Once I broke the metal and plastic case surrounding the keyboard on my typewriter.

One day a coworker saw a hole in the wall near the floor, and she asked me, "Did you do that?"

I turned red with embarrassment. "No, why do you ask?"

She just stared at me and said, "Why do I ask? Because kicking a hole in the wall is exactly the kind of thing you would do."

I told my therapist these stories. He became visibly alarmed and told me to hit a heavy bag at the gym. "You need a safety valve."

I took the suggestion (after I stopped drinking, I was able to take suggestions) and found that I liked hitting a heavy bag while thinking of all the people who pissed me off, from the bullies who tormented me, growing up, to my father, who abandoned me.

Soon just hitting a heavy bag wasn't enough. Within three months, I was taking lessons at the legendary Gleason's boxing gym in Brooklyn. My trainer, Angel, moved me along quickly, to the point where I was ready for my first bout, against a forty-six-year-old money manager renowned for being the oldest man to win a professional fight in New York.

Angel made two mistakes: First, I didn't have a mouth guard. Second, my opponent was insanely aggressive.

I guess the "old guy" wasn't ready for me to fight. I stepped in and rained jabs, rights, and hooks at his head and stomach, pushing him back against the ropes. He quickly regained his composure, counterpunched, and decked me with a clean uppercut that I never saw coming.

I landed on my back, my head bouncing against the canvas floor. Angel jumped into the ring, completely pissed, as the old guy danced around me, shouting, "Yeah, that's how it's done!" in his guttural Brooklyn accent.

Angel yelled at him, helped me up, and told me he was sorry about the mouth guard. He added, "Look, man, it's the punch you don't see that knocks you out." I staggered off to the showers and got dressed. My jaw ached, and there was a ringing in my ears for the next two days.

I was undeterred. Next Saturday morning, I was back, with the cacophony of bells ringing their three-minute rounds, the thwacking of the heavy bags, and the gunfire rotation of the speed bags. In the corner, amateur wrestlers practiced diving off the ropes onto each other with a sudden crash. I loved it. I realized that Norman Mailer was right: Boxing is hard, not because you have to overcome your fear of getting hurt, but because you have to get over the fear of hurting someone else.

A few years later, I almost broke my nose in a white-collar boxing match at Kingsway gym in Manhattan. Another uppercut, this time right on the nose. I didn't go down, but the referee stopped the match when the deep-mahogany-colored blood from my nose spattered onto the canvas floor. I wandered back to the locker room, where my only solace was a visit by ex-heavyweight fighter Michael Grant. He said, "Hey, man, you gotta move your head. Gotta move your head."

That was many years ago, and I still have to work to contain my anger. Now I realize that my feelings were the tail that wagged the dog. I couldn't live with them. Other people seem to manage fear, loneliness, and disappointment without having to kill them with a chemical or raging at someone or something. It's as if I were born without the ability to process certain feelings, and I'm still overwhelmed by them today.

It's too easy to pin all the anger on my father's disappearing act or my mother's alcoholism. A degree of pain will be with me forever. It's more formless than that, to be restless, irritable, and discontent unless I'm getting my way all the time. So I go to a meeting, or meditate, or talk about my current predicament to a friend in recovery. I've come to realize that no matter how I feel, I shouldn't take it too seriously, because three hours from now, I'll feel differently.

I didn't know that when I was drinking.

What I felt is what I was.

24

Relapse Dessert

Except for two occasions—both of which I count as accidental (although others might not)—I didn't have a drink for a
decade.

The first of these errant drinks was a martini on the rocks dis-
guised as a glass of sparkling water that a flight attendant served
me by mistake. I'd ordered a Pellegrino, so it was an easy mistake
to make. For both of us. I took a drink, and ah! Was this an old,
familiar taste blooming on my tongue? But I ordered a Pellegrino
. . . should I take another sip to be certain it isn't? I mean, could I
be wrong? Is this drink mineral water and it's only my imagination
that says it's gin? I should taste it again, perhaps.

Yeah, sure. It requires such a lot of tasting to spot the difference.
Well, I didn't, bless my little alcoholic heart. Good Lord, anyone
with even a smidgen of ability to rationalize could have had that
drink down her throat without any debate. Like a heart attack:

If you think you might be having one, don't stop to figure out whether it is or isn't. Call an ambulance. If you think you might be drinking a martini, don't call the flight attendant, she's the one who brought it in the first place. If you've started drinking, just carry on. Might as well, since a relapse is a relapse.

But oh, no. That year I spent in the clinic—more like two—well, let's say that extra nine months, yes, those months have closed the happy escape route, the languorous path I may never walk again. The steel jaws of the Kolmac Clinic really closed around my own poor jaw (clang-clang!) to the point where I couldn't take even one forgivable sip.

The flight attendant whisked back up the aisle, carrying a tray of potent-looking drinks that sent up fumes of every liquorish scent imaginable, the high note being rum. From my single sip of gin had blossomed a whole seductive drinking world; the sip had almost dropped me down in the gardens of Combray with Proust, whose spoonful of tea and madelene had the town and all of its associations springing up around him. Yes, Proust had his way of seeing that drink of tea through to its end. And his end was glorious.

Well, I had mine, and mine was anything but. That was why I had it. Not that I invented this way of seeing things, no. As far as I'm concerned, the best way of keeping yourself from having the second drink (or even the paltry second sip) is seeing the first one through to its end. Although we know the scenario, how it can end in total drunkenness and crazy behavior; how it comes with blackouts and hangovers; how we can end up facedown on floors and sidewalks, still we stop short in our imagination. When alcoholics think of that first drink, they see the look of it, the liquid silver of vodka, the velvet brown of a beer or a bourbon, feel it in the mouth and throat, and stop short. Having glamorized the first drink, you don't think of the second, the third, the fourth that you would drink, too, and on to the end: depression that comes with yet another failure to control the drinking, and so on. You don't think of all this when you visualize that first drink: You don't see it through to the end.

This is what has kept me from drinking, seeing a drink to its inevitable end. I don't think of the first drink and then stop. No, I know where it leads.

The second alcoholic event took place in a cozy French restaurant on Martha's Vineyard (these scenes are indelibly engraved in the mind, while all of the others—ocean? dunes? gingerbread houses of Oak Bluffs, white brick of Edgartown?—fade away). On the dessert menu was zabaglione, one of my all-time favorites. Yum.

It arrived in a glass as tall as an iceberg, and I dug right in. My eyes opened smartly. How had I forgotten one of the chief (and there are only *three*) ingredients of zabaglione is marsala wine? This chef didn't hold back on it, either. After I tasted it, if anyone thought I wasn't going to eat the rest—ha!

My nose fumed delightfully. It was good to the last spoonful. Or the last drop. And don't think I didn't order it again the next time I patronized that restaurant.

Yes, I would give up the zabaglione about as soon as I'd give up the nitrous oxide that made my visits to the dentist such a positive experience. People questioned this at the clinic, the wisdom of the nitrous. Getting a root canal with the aid of nitrous oxide, I said, is better than sucking on balloons at a Grateful Dead concert, isn't it?

These were my only lapses. Did they qualify as relapse? Though I doubt that accidental sip did, I'm not so sure about the dessert. To make zabaglione, one tosses egg yolks, sugar, and marsala wine in a pan and cooks it over hot water, a double boiler, or some such pot. Cooks it. Now, if it actually cooked the wine, that would mean the marsala's ability to have me sliding from my chair to the floor and passing out was negligible.

Supposedly, in cooking, alcohol burns off. At least that's the received wisdom, and that's what the clinic said. But I did a little research and found that it depends on how you cook the food that the alcohol is added to—boil? simmer? bake? flambé? In some cases, you burn off only 10 percent; in other cases, 85 percent. Since zabaglione isn't supposed to cook much (it would scramble the eggs), I couldn't work out how much alcohol would be tossed to the wind. Of course, one takes into account how long the dish cooks. For zabaglione, it seems to take forever; one has to keep whisking and whisking away at this custard so it doesn't separate. (Given all of that effort, one needs a drink, finally.) Although the custard doesn't really simmer, since it's off the heat, it stays heated up for a long time.

Naturally, I did this research only after I left Martha's Vineyard, lest it jeopardize my visits to the restaurant.

What, then, constitutes a relapse? I believe at least one of our group went off on a bender, and we allowed as how, yes, that sounded as if he'd relapsed. But a woman in the group relapsed with one glass of sherry. That seemed a terrible waste of a relapse, as it wasn't even her tipple.

When I heard the relapse rate is 75 or 80 percent, I was stunned. How on earth did relapsing pass me by? Eighty percent! I doubt those relapses were occupied with a dish of zabaglione.

I found it irritating that the clinic didn't make more of a fuss about the relapse rate. They easily could have framed it in the sense of: "Be prepared!" I would have taken it in the sense of "Let's go!" If there's 80 percent of anything, I'm in line for it. I had to hear this statistic after eleven or twelve years of sobriety, after the parade had passed on by. I thought the relapse rate was more like 2 percent, or perhaps 5 percent, meaning hardly anyone ever relapsed, and if I did, the shame visited on me would have me standing in a corner like that poor fellow at the end of *The Blair Witch Project*.

How is it that I overlooked the fact that when I left the clinic (in a huff, probably) after my first stint, I, well, relapsed, didn't I?

All I can say is, I'm glad I went to that restaurant and had that zabaglione before I went back to the clinic. After all, they'd nearly ruined my trips to the dentist.

25

Fathers and Sons

I don't know if some kids wake up in the morning and suddenly know exactly what they want to do: "I want to be a doctor. I want to be a lawyer. I want to be a dentist." I do know that no one wakes up and says: "I want to be an alcoholic."

I'm descended from a line of men from Georgia with a poor track record of husbanding, fathering, and controlling their drinking. My paternal great-grandfather was told at the turn of the century that if he didn't quit drinking, he'd die. He promptly went out on a bender and fell over dead at the age of thirty-eight. He left a widow and eight children—the second to youngest being my grandfather—and although my great-grandmother remarried eventually, she was turned mean by her circumstances. She was legendary for her tobacco chewing and for horse-whipping any child who got out of line.

My grandfather hated her and ran away to join the army when he was seventeen, forming a love-hate relationship with the armed forces that lasted the rest of his life. He was defiant of authority and conformity yet in love with travel and adventure. When my grandmother wouldn't sign the papers to let him reenlist during World War II because he was the sole provider for their four children, he promptly found a way around that with the Merchant Marines. The Merchant Marines didn't require her signature. He spent the last year of the war ferrying materials to England and sailing around the world.

Some of my grandfather's brothers and sisters drank, but no one as much as he did.

Frustrated with his life, hemmed in by his family, an active alcoholic who was clinically depressed, he killed himself at fifty-two. In 1949 he put his head in the gas oven in the kitchen. He addressed the suicide note to my father, the youngest of four and a freshman at a small liberal arts college in Tennessee. My grandfather survived longer than his father did, but he still left behind a widow and four children between the ages of seventeen and twenty-two.

Among my father's three siblings, he was the only alcoholic, although the damage done by his father's suicide reverberated through the whole family for decades. The two surviving sisters blamed their mother for their father's suicide, treating her abysmally, not visiting her except for perfunctory holiday stopovers. My grandmother persevered. She took it all stoically and even laughed about her daughters' selfish behavior. After she survived the Great Depression by picking cotton while her husband went north to look for work, nothing could shake her.

On May 29, 1990, I sat and stared at a photo of the grandfather I never knew, an impossibly young man gazing hopefully in his World War I–era army uniform. I wanted to follow his path. I stood up, walked two steps over to the kitchen—it was a New York City apartment—opened the oven, turned on the gas, and stuck my head in. I lasted for five seconds. I pulled my head out, turned off the gas, and went over to the window—I lived on the tenth floor—opened the window, and threw one leg over the sill. I looked down at the garbage cans piled up in front of the basement door behind my building. I sat and looked at the Empire State Building shining white in that never quite dark New York City sky. This lasted less than ten seconds. I pulled myself back in and sat on the couch, disgusted that I couldn't even kill myself.

My life was over. I was twenty-five years old.

My connection to the men who preceded me began with my parents' separation and then divorce. I was under two. My mother left my father because his drinking and erratic behavior were affecting her mental health. He eventually left the small college in Maryland where they were English teachers, and went to graduate school at Indiana University.

I was too young to remember my mother kicking my father out of the house, but I do have vague memories of visiting him a few times when he was still drinking. He never got another full-time teaching job. He was irregular with employment and child support until he landed the alcoholic's dream job, with the Red Cross—all drama and no commitment. For three years he traveled across the country, playing the hero—flying into disaster sites for two to four weeks at a time, helping the locals during the day while drinking heavily in their bars at night.

Even being single, with no responsibilities, could not save my father from his own alcoholism. He got sick and tired of being sick and tired and got sober in Baltimore in 1970. He magically reappeared in my life when I turned six, with no explanation, and tried to make up for lost time. There was no explanation for his absence, no mea culpa, nothing. I was too scared to ask any questions in case he went away again. I just tried to forget not seeing him for years, and buried the anger so I could enjoy any attention he gave me. I couldn't talk to my mother about it because she was still angry for what he'd put us through. I sensed an internal wall about those years that I couldn't break through.

Over the next few years, he made more of an effort to visit and have me stay with him after he moved out of his mother's apartment into his own two rooms. By the time I was nine years old, we scheduled visits every other weekend, and in his limited way, my father tried his best to be a good parent. My most vivid memories are of him reading to me in a big square chair with wide arms. I would sit and pick at the polyester upholstery as he read me C. S. Lewis's Narnia series, *Huckleberry Finn, The Three Musketeers,* and other classic children's books.

Another passion my father and I shared was the Baltimore Orioles. The 1970s and early 1980s were a great time for the team at the old redbrick Memorial Stadium. Section 34 was where the rowdy, self-anointed Orioles cheerleader "Wild" Bill whipped fans into a frenzy with his "O!R!I!O!L!E!S!" chant. I loved the excitement, the fans smoking cigarettes and drinking beer, the ceremonial burning of the pennants of the hated New York Yankees and Boston Red Sox, the booing of Reggie Jackson. I even loved the corny fan sing-along to Kenny Rogers's first major hit, "Lucille," in the steamy Maryland twilight. Lucille was my grandmother's name.

Today my father has outlived his father by almost thirty years. My grandfather made it to fifty-two, fourteen years longer than his father. My father is eighty years old. He is a survivor, but he remains a mystery to me and, I think, a mystery to himself.

Whatever doors he closed and walls he erected to survive have created limitations that have often stopped me cold over the decades. I've wondered: Is it that he can't or won't? We share a love of reading and politics and baseball, but little else of what interests me interests him. He lived in the same tiny one-bedroom apartment for twenty-six years, next door to his mother in a broken-down blue-collar Baltimore suburb that he could have left decades ago. He has never evinced any interest in exploring or stretching out of his comfort zone. He never travels for pleasure, has little ambition, and seems disinterested in how he lives. If he can't reach out beyond those limitations because of what he had to survive growing up, I understand. I'll never know the answer. We have talked many times, and he paints a picture of an idyllic childhood that I don't believe.

With my two sons, I've tried to be the opposite. If anything, I have erred the other way, revving too high and loading on too many family activities. I try to avoid any painful feelings by organizing a frenzied schedule of activities—multiple museum visits, nature excursions, sports activities, and day trips to monuments. One of my best friends in recovery nicknamed me "Mr. Blur."

"Onward to Mount Vernon . . . time to climb Sugarloaf Mountain . . . wait, there's a play to see at the Kennedy Center . . . but let's not forget the art museum!"

My sons have never seen me drunk, and I hope that makes a difference in their lives. It's a gamble of the genetic dice for them.

Hopefully a completely different environment than the one I grew up in and the one my father grew up in will make a difference. I hope they are spared a disease that has afflicted four generations of men in my family.

I hope the disease ends with me. I hope the sins of the fathers aren't passed down to my sons.

THIRD CONVERSATION:
ADDICTION, DISEASE, AND ANONYMITY

KG: In January 2011, a writer for *Harper's* magazine who is now sober broke multiple rules with regard to the traditions for twelve-step meetings by discussing specific meetings, naming people at the meetings, and reporting what they said. He mentioned in a meeting how his psychiatrist had him on medications for depression. A silence fell on the meeting. My experience is that sometimes there is an uneasy alliance between those in the program who do not take medication and those who take it for anxiety, clinical depression, and other mental illness.

In the vast majority of meetings I've gone to, this isn't an issue. In the twelve-step literature, it clearly states that we are not doctors and that people should go to see doctors for "problems other than alcohol." But at some meetings there is a faction of the old guard who got sober when these drugs were not available, so they're suspicious of using pills to alter the brain chemistry and make one feel better. They are hostile toward psychiatry because, for so many years, psychiatrists and therapists knew little about alcoholism and took their money, and it was a complete waste of time for everyone. There's a saying—"Analysis is paralysis"—that I used to hear in meetings. It didn't mean psychiatric analysis. It meant trying to get to the greater truth. Trying to analyze and discover *why* you drink will only get you drunker. There is no answer. Trying to figure out the whys is useless.

To be fair to the psychiatric profession, the alcoholics in treatment would lie about their drinking, thus making their addiction hard to diagnose.

MG: So in meetings you've been to, it doesn't matter if people mention their therapists or psychiatrists?

KG: Not at all. But I avoid—and I think many others in meetings do as well—mentioning them, because that's not what we're here to talk about; we're here to talk about recovery, the steps, not what our therapists said about our childhoods. I can't stand people who, for example, share their dreams. That's not what I'm there for.

MG: I think you're caught up in a number of clichés, or perhaps "brainwashings" would be a better way of putting it. "Analysis paralysis" is one way of jettisoning both formal analysis and self-analysis. I agree completely that to think you can stop drinking by starting with analysis is a mistake. But to say that analysis is useless is, well, idiotic. You also say one thing, then another: Yes, there is an uneasy alliance between members who have therapists and/or take drugs; later, you say that there is no prejudice at all about members who do this. You can get out of it by saying the tone of meetings differs. I doubt there's a difference except in degree of mistrust. I agree that if a lot of members in therapy start talking about what's going on, discussion could get so tangled up (as in recounting dreams) that it would be worthless.

On the other hand, I believe that if you lined up a lot of veteran A.A. members, they'd turn thumbs down on psychiatry, with the objection that it roots around in the past and isn't useful. That's a stereotype and a cliché. I also think it hints at A.A.'s holier-than-thou attitude.

KG: Sure, maybe it's holier than thou, but we're talking about a life-threatening disease.

MG: I have a problem with alcoholics constantly defining themselves by their disease.

KG: One of the most important findings of recovery is that if you can permit yourself to say that alcoholism is a disease, you escape the shame that is too often associated with drinking. The old notion of the town drunk, the falling-down man in a raincoat rolling in the gutter in the Bowery: These kinds of images still exist for people, even in our *Oprah* age. I look at alcoholism as a disease, and the main symptom is an inability to stop drinking to the point where it causes death.

On the other hand, I have a friend, a molecular biologist, who claims that if he can't see it on a slide, it isn't a disease.

MG: I agree with him. How can you group addiction with cancer, heart problems, stroke, measles, tuberculosis? To say that drinking is a disease because if you carry on with it long enough, you could die, is hardly logical. You're saying if you drink hard enough, long enough, you could die. That's true, but you can't say disease is the cause. The disease concept does, I guess, take away the onus of having to accept responsibility.

KG: So do you prefer the allergy concept? Do you believe the causes of addiction have a physical component?

MG: No, I don't believe in the allergy concept any more than I believe in the measles and mumps concept. Oh, there's a physical component, yes, in the way your brain processes the drugs. It's important for the medical community to classify addiction as a disease because of health insurance.

If it's a disease, your insurance pays for treatment. The American Medical Association kicked the disease thing around for a long time, didn't it? For example, I don't drink anymore, so would people in recovery think I still have the disease?

KG: In the eyes of a lot of people in recovery, you would probably be considered "dry." Meaning that you're physically sober, but you would have to make your own judgment as to whether you're emotionally sober. Emotional sobriety depends on your having some kind of contact with the Higher Power idea, and the ability to accept your situation with a degree of serenity. Some semblance of peace of mind instead of suffering from RIDS—Restless, Irritable, and Discontent.

In my experience, most alcoholics have a compulsion to control their environment. For example, I have read that as many as one out of three women in recovery have eating disorders. The desire to control everything in the external world, to gamble or overeat (or not eat), is connected with a greater malaise, or illness, which is an essential dissatisfaction with the way the world is, with the way people are, that disappointment is a frequent unwanted guest. There's nothing we can do but accept it.

MG: Wait a minute—you realize you're talking about the entire population. Everyone's dissatisfied with the way the world is—

KG: Yes, but they don't deal with it by drinking four or five martinis or a fifth of Jim Beam or a couple of six-packs a day. We're talking about a very specific way of dealing with the outside world. An alcoholic keeps the refrain going: "I don't fit in, I don't like the way the world works, why aren't people more the way I want them to be? Fuck it, I'm going to drink."

People who aren't alcoholics have all of the same feelings; they just don't get to the "Fuck it, I'm going to drink" part. They say, "Well, I hope this ends soon," or "I'm going to call a friend and have dinner"—something like that, which consoles them to the degree that they don't lash out self-destructively at the world.

MG: God, I find it hard to believe that all those who aren't addicts deal with their problems in such a healthy way. I don't think they do. I think they have fights with their partners and yell at the kids. I mean, really—

KG: Wait, though. These thoughts about life have a finality and a totality for alcoholics, a sense that nothing can ever change, that this will go on forever. When they stop drinking and they're physically dried out, they can come to see who and what they are. By going through the twelve steps, they begin to see their flaws and defects. They share this with somebody else to get relief from the guilt over the things they've done—and not done—while drinking, the same guilt that made them keep drinking and not quit. Then they make amends—and by amends, I don't mean simply saying "I'm sorry" but really acknowledging it. They do this by paying back loans, or being of service to other people, or changing longtime aberrant behaviors for those around them. This is a cycle that should raise you out of a self-pitying, victimized worldview. Like that Chet Baker song "Everything Happens to Me." I bet if I played that song at a meeting, everyone would laugh, because every alcoholic has felt exactly that way most of the time they were drinking, and maybe half the time when they were sober.

That's what the twelve steps are trying to get to: Bottles are but a symbol. Drinking is a symptom. It's what's underneath that it's trying to change. People in recovery believe that if you don't do the steps, you're vulnerable to drinking—

MG: That's what you believe.

KG: Yes, I do. Now, that's not to say there aren't issues that complicate all of this—clinical depression, for instance. Twelve-step programs believe that practicing the steps will lead to the priceless gift of serenity. If you can get to that place, picking up a drink won't occur to you. But if you're a victim, and everybody's out to get you, and things are driving you crazy, why not drink?

MG: Look, if I had the "priceless gift of serenity," obviously, I wouldn't need to drink. But if I'm a victim, why not drink, you say? Because I wouldn't be able to stop. Now, your sometimes smug twelve-stepper would say I'm emotionally dry because I'm not doing the steps—

KG: You're right, you're not doing the steps, and I think you would be happier if you did.

MG: I don't. I think A.A. is a great institution because it offers something that is indeed priceless: fellowship. Even so, I think the twelve steps are dumb, except for the first one, which is the important one, which is the *only* one, which is the one that will get you from here to there. Admit you are powerless over alcohol. It's the leap of faith. The cavern you're crossing is denial. Indeed, they're like two sides of the same coin: faith and denial. Neither one can be explained in rational terms; they both defy rationality.

26

WebDrunk

In a book titled *The Shallows,* Nicholas Carr writes about the effects of the Internet on the way we perceive things. He says that the Web has completely changed the way he does research. He used to refer to books; now he goes online. He notices that it has become increasingly difficult for him to read books. And friends he's talked to who have for some time been poring over the Web for research, instead of poring over books, have found that they can no longer read books. It has become almost impossible for them to sustain the concentration necessary to read printed pages. These people have been doing research through books for years, but now they can't train their attention on printed material.

The author's point is that arguments about the pros and cons of what the Web gives us are nearly always centered on content: how crass it is, how shallow and superficial. But content, Carr says, isn't the problem. The problem is the delivery system, in this case the Web, and what it does to the way we read what's on the screen; that is, the way we perceive the content.

This is important. It hearkens back to Marshall McLuhan's famous dictum, "The medium is the message." The message is changed by the way it is delivered. The delivery system embeds itself in the message.

Take the way the Web gives us news and how it differs from the way traditional newspapers convey it. The screen breaks up into pictures, photos, colors, sounds that convey pieces of information running in different directions. Advertisements pop up, images throb. There is constant, often dizzying motion.

In the 1960s, McLuhan predicted the "end of the linear mind."

We've grown so used to getting our information via the Internet that we're demanding that delivery system more and more. Why else would a newspaper such as *The Washington Post* change its format from linear black on white to imitate a Web page? Every byline now has a photo of the journalist accompanying it. We demand pictures.

People are giving up newspapers because they lack the juice, the quick and colored fragments, the eye-spring of the page that makes our eyes dart back and forth—one could say the way in which we read the page, yet one wonders what kind of reading is going on.

At the same time, I'm reading a book on Buddhism that says, "Don't get caught up in the content." I need to empty my mind. This is difficult. I always get caught up in the content.

What has this to do with addiction? I have a suspicion that twelve-step programs are about the medium, not about the content.

Form, the delivery system, might be vital to success here, when content is given all the credit.

Take the slogans: They're short; they're sweet; they're easy to absorb. They're supposedly to the point (I wonder sometimes what point). "Easy Does It," "One Day at a Time," "Keep It Simple, Stupid." They don't ask you to think about what they say; indeed, they don't want you to think about it. (Although one of the slogans is "Think," I don't believe it. It goes against the sloganeering grain, and perhaps against the content grain, since alcoholics are constantly reminded not to think too much, not to analyze the problem.) The slogans are accepted en masse. They are not questioned; they are not held up to the light to see what's behind them.

I'm not criticizing this. The method—the delivery system—the slogan is probably necessary for success. We're being told: Do not think about it. Ordinarily, I would say this is bad advice, but not in this case. Remember that the purpose of the twelve-step program is to get you to stop drinking (or otherwise drugging). The purpose is not to get you to understand why you do it and then stop.

I've often wondered how successful interventions can be because relatives and friends intervening have to reason with the addict. For instance, they tell him how he's causing pain to each of them; how he's endangering his health; how drugs are affecting his work. The addict, the center of it all, looks around with shifty-eyed sincerity.

The problem is the content: how you've hurt us, how you're hurting yourself, et cetera. In other words, the same rationality that's always brought to bear is present here. What if the ones intervening paid more attention to form? I don't think it's content at work, since that can appeal only to the rational mind, which the addict is sorely lacking, or else the content is something he already knows. Content is a list of things the alcoholic has done and is doing. Content is "Remember the dinner where you threw a drink in my face?" The medium, the delivery system, is the person presenting the message, the look on his face, perhaps the way he leans forward in his chair.

At least that's what I think must be happening. I don't think addicts respond to content. Those rhetorical questions asked during an intervention—"Can't you see what your drinking is doing to your family?"—are content. But the way in which they're asked, or the person doing the asking, is the medium.

The message lies in the medium. The way you say something is actually what you say.

Ask any poet.

27

MG

Reading Robert Parker

I'm reading Robert B. Parker's latest book. His dialogue is a lesson in economy and precision. No sentence is left unsharpened.

Spenser, Parker's favorite character, and a lady friend are sitting in a bar with a great view. She orders a lemon-drop martini. I don't know what that is.

"Smooths out a day," she says, taking a sip.

I do know what that is.

She drinks her lemon-drop martini, and Spenser drinks beer.

And I drink nothing.

I bought this book for somebody else, a big Spenser fan, and picked it up because I wanted to escape a Sunday sadness.

It's not much of an escape, because I want to crawl into Robert B. Parker's pages, into this lounge, and join Spenser and the woman sipping the lemon-drop martini.

It occurs to me that Robert Parker might have been a drinker, not necessarily of notable proportions, but a man who might have stopped drinking once or twice and then gone back to it. I wonder, Why can't I do that? I'm old enough to be dead, so why am I not old enough to hang out in a cocktail lounge? Why can't I join these people, or no people, in a bar and have a martini? Even a lemon-drop one, which sounds more fey than good, but who cares? It's what the lemon drop is dropped in.

You think I'm going to come up with a really good reason for not joining Spenser and his friend? Sorry to disappoint, but I'm not. I don't have a really good reason. That, you might think, is pretty unsettling, pretty lame, considering all the pages I've inked up with reasons not to drink.

I can't come up with a better one at the moment other than that I don't have any vodka in the house. But that's no problem, is it, since a bottle of Grey Goose is as easily acquired in D.C. as a handgun.

It's easy enough to pop out to the liquor store, easier still to walk into any of the thousand restaurants in revitalized Bethesda, plunk myself down, and have drinks before dinner (I think that's what Spenser and the blonde are doing).

"A martini—wait, make that a double, on the rocks." Hold the lemon drops.

Nearly every alcoholic who stops goes back to it at least once and probably several times. So why can't I join Spenser? Why can't I be part of this larger, looser, lusher life? Sit in a restaurant with a martini before dinner? Or join my friends down at Swill's, or the neighbors at a Friday-evening cocktail party? Or the serene and padded lounge patronized by Spenser? Places where you can get down; you can unwind; you can be yourself, escape the feeling of exclusion and separateness.

Or can you?

I thought you could until I read an article in *The New Yorker* about what happens to the sense of exclusion that, sober, you feel so painfully. Drinking excludes you even more. You become less, not more, yourself; you become more, not less, isolated. The sense of dissolving boundaries is an illusion.

But I'm compelled to drink, so I construct a narrative to dress up the compulsion. The narrative spins out of the glass; the narrative is "connection."

E. M. Forster said: "Only connect." I find that writing will sometimes do it, give me that sense of connection with the world. Hauling a little kid out of a burning building might do it. Climbing the north face of the Eiger might do it. Meditation might do it. These things erase or at least soften the boundaries between us and the world outside.

I always thought taking a drink would do it.

That, though, is probably the illusion of all illusions. It's also the only thing in the list above that requires no effort. None at all. Could that be a telling point when it comes to connecting?

I have a wardrobe of illusions. I'm sure, hanging in some closet, there is one that embraces British pubs. Pubs always seemed to me the quintessential drinking places. If you visit a particular pub most nights, you'll see the same faces. There is a feeling of homeyness, and for good reason: Pubs are extensions of home.

Dr. Kolodner once said it was interesting (meaning suspicious) that I named my books after pubs. I said that I could never think up a title more interesting than a pub called The Man with a Load of Mischief or Help the Poor Struggler.

Ha ha. He didn't say that, but it's probably what he was thinking. After I stopped drinking, I found it awfully hard to go into pubs and sit with a glass of San Pellegrino where once I sat with a glass of Guinness.

Pubs, I said to Dr. Kolodner, are far more than places in which to drink. There's atmosphere; there's history . . .

Ha ha, he didn't say.

But he was probably (ha ha) right: my fascination with pubs had to do with more than the names, or the pub's place in the social scheme of British life. I liked pubs because I could drink in them. The mismatched tables and chairs, the accents of the voices, the stuff on the walls—old churches, old villages, old dogs—the drink in my hand.

The drink in my hand.

The rest of it was a romantic construct, essentially an illusion.

Why, then, can't I join Spenser in a drink?

There is an answer both literal and metaphorical.

Because he isn't there.

28

KG

—

The Child of the Writer's Life

One of the most powerful memories I have is of my mother at her desk, typing furiously at eighty words a minute, while taking flight in a world of her own making. I can recall watching her drink tea while she read Henry James and Jane Austen and Charles Dickens, and listening to her groan while grading her students' papers. But it was looking at her writing that I remember most vividly. The smell of the fresh paper, the ink ribbons, her hair moving as her hands flew across the keys. It was hypnotic. I was there with her, but she was very far away, someplace else, where I couldn't be.

Growing up with a writer, or any artist, is different. The passion she feels for her art creates a distance that often can't be breached. My mother wasn't rejecting me, though many times I couldn't pierce the zone of impenetrability that surrounded her and her writing. I was amazed by how smart she was, and I desperately tried to keep up with her; I knew she wasn't like the other moms in kitchens making dinner, or in parlors dusting furniture, or coming back from the store with a carload of groceries. My mother did all those things while keeping up a nonstop stream of commentary that made me constantly laugh out loud. She was much funnier than those other moms, and her moods were harder to read.

It was like a carousel spun out of control. She was trying to teach her underachieving college students while writing, shuttling me from one school to another, with the single parent's constant financial pressure. I rode this carousel, uncertain what might make her angry or frustrated.

I had no brothers or sisters and saw my father sporadically, so my mother was all I had. My dependence on her increased when we moved from one house or state or country to another. I remember once in England, when I was ten, devising cunning tape-and-water-tray traps in front of doors to capture her because she spent so many hours writing and reading Jane Austen and Henry James.

My mother had friends but was a very private person, and we spent much of our time alone. I enjoyed being by myself sometimes (and still do), but as I grew older, I became outgoing and focused on being popular. I realize now that much of my self-worth was derived by what other kids (and, later, adults) thought of me.

After Christmas 1974, we moved from suburban Washington, D.C., to Denmead, a tiny village near Portsmouth in Hampshire, England. There wasn't much to do in the village, and there was no one to play with. It was here, when I was ten, that I fell in love with books and used them to escape into a fantasy world. I read and reread Lewis Carroll, Greek mythology, and scores of Hardy Boys and Nancy Drew mysteries.

We arrived after Christmas, and my mother decided I would

finish fourth grade in Denmead. We walked into the headmaster's office in the beginning of January, and I registered as a student. Why, halfway through the school year, they took a kid from America whose mother was renting a house in the village, I never could understand.

The school was an ordinary elementary school on the edge of our ordinary English village with its High Street, where I would buy comic books at the tobacconist. The architecture was post–World War II redbrick buildings, and the fields around the school were lush and green. With the cloudy skies and the chilly spring weather, Denmead was the epitome of Englishness.

There were about two hundred village kids who largely ignored my arrival. The teachers made no special effort for me. The greatest interest shown in me was one day the principal eyed me suspiciously and pulled me into his office, demanding that I stop a "funny walk" I was using in the hallways. I had no idea what he was talking about.

I dutifully went to class and did my work and tried my best to understand the metric system. I had to grit my teeth during sports when the football (soccer) coach kept referring to me as "Mr. Nixon" in front of the whole class, eliciting sniggers from the fourth-grade boys. The English think they're funny, wry, witty, and like to "take the piss" out of people, particularly foreigners. What really bothered me was that during the daily football class, they didn't try to teach us how to play through drills. The coach just assumed that by age ten, all of the kids knew the rules and knew how to play. Since I had never played football, they immediately put me in the goal, where I could do no damage. Rarely was a ball launched my way, and I quickly understood that I had been given the loser position. I would lean against the metal-frame goalpost and watch the other kids pass the ball in the middle of the field, far in the distance on the regulation-sized pitch.

One day when I came home from school, I told my mother how much I hated it there. As she drank her tea, I blurted out everything about the school that I didn't like. There was nothing to be done—I had to finish up the fourth grade in England.

This was the beginning of a pattern that continues to this day. I would let things build and not talk at all about what was happening to me, hopeless that anything would change. Sometimes my unhappiness would spill out, but more often I kept it to myself. A hallmark of alcoholism is the refusal to share your real feelings of loneliness with anyone.

The situation at school did not improve. The English are not known for their warmth or kindness to strangers, and most of the kids stared at me and kept their distance. I made a few friends. I read and stared at my mother's back as she attacked her typewriter and finished her first novel.

My mother had switched from writing poetry to short stories and then novels. I didn't understand why she made me switch, but I really enjoyed her first novel. Perhaps this was because I could understand it; her poetry was too hard for me. I could appreciate the adventures of her character Leonard, an English teacher who hooks up with a bunch of misfits and turns thief. It was something I could sink my teeth into.

Our cottage was a classic two-bedroom with a thatched roof and plaster walls. In my tiny bedroom, where the typewriter was set up, my mother would loudly bang out words at an exhilarating pace, then hand the pages to me to read as I sat behind her.

How could my mom be here in front of me but in a world of her imagination? How could she come up with all of these characters? How could she be so funny? She seemed happy when she was writing, happier than when she stepped away from the typewriter and back to the drudgery of washing clothes, making dinner, and being responsible for me with no help. How could I ever measure up to her talent and patience and perseverance? And how could I ever stand to be alone long enough to create a work of fiction?

The answer is, I couldn't.

29

Things Lurk

I think people enjoy believing writers are alcoholics; it makes the whole idea of writing for a living even edgier, more daring, and hence, more romantic.

I could almost say I drank the way I wrote: determinedly. Persistently. I was a maintenance drinker. Nothing flashy, nothing flamboyant. (I have a suspicion that Hemingway and Fitzgerald were not maintenance drinkers.)

When I started in publishing, it felt like a cottage industry; there was a smallness to it, a sense of fraternity, of family. It was spoken of as a gentlemen's industry. I'm sure there are still gentlemen, and there's still something personal about it, but that's hard to find under the weight of German, Dutch, and French conglomerates, huge chain bookstores, and Amazon (what a fitting name).

I taught in college and wrote at the same time. That was in the late 1970s, when people at publishing houses read unsolicited manuscripts (those unrepresented by an agent). It was also a time when the terms "memoir" and "debut novel" were missing from the lexicon (a blessing, but there went half the playing field).

I sent my first manuscript to one publisher at a time and waited until it came back (with its rejection slip) before sending it to another. On and on. What I remember most was my persistence. Dogged determination. Did I know the book would be published? Of course not. Why would I need to be doggedly determined if I knew that?

The trouble is, no matter what you endeavor to do, what plan you undertake, down that road you're going, things lurk: to distract you, to scare you, to convince you that you're useless or at best on the wrong road—get off!

Things always lurk. Behind the tree, squatting in the bushes, on the edge of the field or the lake.

If writing is the road you want to go, you need only two things: persistence and the desire to tell a story. You don't have to believe you're talented or even very smart. You don't have to think you're a good person or devoted to anything. You don't have to be anything but conscious and determined.

Right here, as I'm concentrating hard, three lawn mowers have started up. It sounds like a bullet train is bearing down, and I shoot out of my chair, blood in my eye. I'm going to kill Roberto, the gardener who's popped up from the bushes.

You can say, Oh, poor you; I wish I had a big enough lot to need three lawn mowers. Now, in addition to the lost concentration, I'm feeling guilty because I have a huge lot. I am stopped cold by this, and now I'll have to rev myself up all over again to get the concentration back, to get to that point on the road where I can write.

Don't think, when this happens, that you can complain to others about the interruption, because they won't know what you're talking about. (After all, it didn't do me any good to complain to you, did it?) If you think life is set against you, that it's a giant computer screen with stuff you don't want to see popping up all over, competing for your attention—you're absolutely right.

Here is where the fabled cabin in the woods looks grand. It makes a drink look grand, too. (Who am I kidding? Anything could make a drink look grand.) There will always be an excuse for not writing, just as there will always be an excuse for drinking. *I can't write until I can get away to that cabin in the woods, that shack by the sea, that retreat, that sanctuary. that escape from distraction . . .*

Here comes Max in his monster suit. Remember Max? He got put to bed early for misbehaving. After a while, his mom relents and brings him a steaming bowl of soup.

Max is not interested in soup. He wants control over everything, like a king. Max cannot control his mom, so he takes himself off to the land of the Wild Things. Hideous (sort of) monsters. Max, who has his monster suit on, becomes one of them and controls them. They have a great time together, Max and the monsters. They want him to stay forever, but Max thinks it's time for him to be heading home.

Max conjures all of this up within a few minutes; you know it's only minutes, because when he returns home and to bed, his soup is still hot.

Max did all that in minutes.

You can't seem to get down a sentence? Yes, things lurk, like: *I don't have enough talent for this . . . Spelling, my spelling has always been terrible . . . Time for dinner; I haven't cooked it . . . Who am I kidding, thinking I can write a book? . . . There go the lawn mowers again . . .*

I need a drink, boy, but do I ever need a drink! . . . How do you get an agent? . . . Maybe if I had an agent . . . The kids are fighting . . . How am I supposed to concentrate with those damned lawn mowers going? It's impossible to write around here! I need to get off somewhere; I need a cabin in the woods . . .

There will always be monsters.

You be Max.

30

MG

Idiot's Delite

"How many drunks does it take to change the bulb in your ceiling fixture?" asks my witty building manager on Capitol Hill.

"I don't know," I unwittily say. "How many?"

"Depends how many could balance on the chair with you."

(Very funny, Chris.) "Did the people downstairs say something?" I'm a bit anxious about this.

Chris looks at the ceiling. "Not much. Just that they thought a big fight was going on. Things crashing, shouts. That kinda thing." Big crocodile smile.

"Well, yes, I guess the chair did tip over. I'd hardly describe it like they did."

"So you were changing the lightbulb."

"Sure. It burned out when I was fixing dinner."

"At three A.M."

"Well, I tend to eat late."

"Next time invite me. I'm taller. That way, it'd only take one drunk to change the lightbulb."

This little tableau suggested itself because I was thinking over the several times I'd made the statement in and out of clinic meetings that I couldn't remember doing anything drunk-y. I never had blackouts, never forgot anything that happened the night before, never said things that made me cringe in the morning. Rarely had hangovers.

Ah, then the routine with the lightbulb at three A.M. came back to me like a bit of Proust's involuntary memory. That memory accomplished, I dredged around for some more drunken moments. Perhaps there were other curious incidents like the bulb in the nighttime.

As if by magic, I recalled the pie-shaped stairs of the narrow staircase in my house in Bucks County. I'm quite sure I missed my footing once and fell partway down that sinister staircase. Did I spill the martini?

Try as I might (and granted, I'm not trying awfully hard), I can remember no other alcoholic missteps. Then how can you trust me to report correctly? I think it's safe to say I was not a drunk of monumental proportions, like a few writers whose talent I couldn't get within shouting distance of: Raymond Chandler, F. Scott Fitzgerald, Tennessee Williams, John Cheever, Ernest Hemingway, Dorothy Parker.

And then there was the great Raymond Carver.

Raymond Carver was, as he himself said, a "full-time drunk" whose writing got in the way of his drinking. He was in and out of rehabs over a large part of his life. Finally, he was told by his doctor that if he continued drinking, he'd die. Soon. He kept right on drinking.

And then one day Carver decided to stop, and he did.

When asked about his accomplishments, Raymond Carver, one of the greatest short-story writers who ever lived, said that the accomplishment of which he was most proud was that he'd stopped drinking. In an interview in the *Paris Review,* he said, "I'm prouder of that, that I quit drinking, than I am of anything in my life."

If that isn't a testament to sobriety, God knows what is.

31

KG

Allons-y!

The most desolate place I've ever seen is off the coast of Ireland in the Aran Islands. It's called the Wormhole, and it's an image I've been drawn to over and over again.

My mother and I traveled to Ireland the summer I was ten years old, and for a boy my age, there was nothing to do. I couldn't ride a bike that well (I had learned how only a short time before). There were no toys, no shops, only a tiny village with a small boarding-house run by a Gestapo-like owner who barely tolerated children.

The beach wasn't what I was used to in the United States. There was no sand, only rocks; no waves, only chilly, flat water going out to the horizon. It wasn't warm enough to lie in the sun. The far-off, cold, turgid, gray North Sea was something you stared at for its wild beauty.

Time had stopped on the island. It was 1974 but easily could have been 1874.

I was left to explore with two older kids on holiday with their parents. One day we worked our way across the fields of heather toward the ocean and came across the Wormhole. Carved out of the solid rock of the coast, the sea had formed a vast square hole about fifty feet across and forty feet deep. I stood, staring down into the sea, listening to the waves roar against the rocky walls, the swells of the ocean pouring in, wishing I could throw myself down into the waters. The cry of the seagulls and the kids on either side pulled me out of my reverie. The Wormhole has stayed with me to this day—I still feel its downward pull from time to time.

One way to resist that pull is by sheer propulsion. *"Allons-y!"* ("Let's go") is one of my favorite expressions to use with my sons. It expresses determination and hopefulness that the next thing we'll do will be an unforgettable experience. Like my mother taking me to see *2001: A Space Odyssey* when I was nine years old. Or *Gone With the Wind* when I was eight (and again when I was eleven). Or *Richard II* at the Royal Shakespeare Company in Stratford-upon-Avon when I was eleven. These experiences and many others, like traveling to Prague a few years after the 1968 revolution, or driving across Ireland to see the castles became transcendent in the Isle of Sky light. How could the boredom of everyday suburban living compete?

I'm convinced that boredom, or even the fear of boredom, is a big part of my alcoholism. There is a Ph.D. dissertation to be written about boredom's role in drinking, gambling, and womanizing. For me and many drunks, a regular life, as described by Robert De Niro in the film *Heat,* is boring. He says, "If you mean life as ball games and barbecues? I don't think so."

I'm still an excitement junkie. When I moved from New York City back to suburban Maryland, it took me five years to detox from Manhattan and gradually come down from the adrenaline rush of living there.

Recovery is composed of many things. One is simple behavior modification. "Stay away from people, places, and things" you encountered when you were drinking is the advice in recovery. You can't stay sober if you're around the same people, doing the same things in the same places—the combination is too powerful and goads you to drink.

My mother and I would be considered "high bottom" drunks, in the parlance of recovery: I had a job (if barely), and she still had a home. "Low bottom" drunks usually have lost everything and become homeless or imprisoned. My mother's experiences and mine were very different, but the suffering and doubt were enough to make us both want to get sober.

The pull downward represented by the image of the Wormhole has become the polar opposite of my relationship with a Higher Power. The Wormhole is hard to understand, mysterious and remote. My Higher Power is equally mysterious.

Six months before I got sober, I found myself on my knees at the Quaker meetinghouse in New York City. I didn't know why I was there, because I had never believed in God. When the leaders of the meeting asked for visitors to identify themselves, I stood up and said it was my first Quaker meeting in eight years. I went to the coffee hour, and the people seemed polite, but no one showed any interest in why I was there. In my alcoholic grandiosity, they should have been crowding around me, giving me phone numbers and welcoming me. I eventually found that when I finally went to twelve-step meetings, I left discouraged and went home.

The Quakers meet in silence and meditation, looking for the spirit to move them. They attend meeting, not church. It's an

inward-looking religion, not a lecture by a religious authority figure. All of the members are equal. If moved to speak, they can
stand and share anything they like. I've attended Quaker meeting
on and off for many years, volunteered in their homeless shelters,
and continued meditating on my own. Little did I know when I
went to a Quaker high school and blew off silent worship to get
high in the woods that I would end up attending twelve-step meetings that are similar to Quaker meetings: All the members are
equal, no one criticizes you, and you get to choose what you want
to talk about. I've finally agreed with what I heard from an old
Irishman in recovery years ago: The answer to my unhappiness
is a conscious contact with a power greater than myself whom I
choose to call God—"because that's His fucking name."

The image of the Wormhole finally faded from my life a few
years ago, when my wife and kids and I were in Florida visiting
my mother. I decided to charter a boat to go fishing with my family. My uncle had taken me out fishing a few times and taught me
the rudiments, and I had taken my boys fishing in South Carolina
a few times. In the beginning, I wrestled with my own incompe-
tence with the rods, reels, fishing lines, and tackle boxes, while
trying not to lose my temper as the kids constantly asked for help.
It occurred to me that hiring a professional might help, and a char-
tered fishing trip on the Gulf Coast might be just what we needed
to amp up our skill level.

On a beautiful breezy Florida morning, we pushed off with
Captain Tom, an amiable man with the fishing captain's requisite
shades, FSU cap, and plug of chew in his bottom lip. He talked to
us on our way out to the Gulf, pointed out the shore birds flying
by, and regaled us with stories about the mighty marlins and grou-
per he had caught and the kinds of fish we would see.

Captain Tom explained to my seven- and five-year-old boys some very basic rules. We are catch-and-release fishermen—my sons are vegetarians—and Captain Tom laid down the rules. "After you catch the fish, never pull it into the boat. If you have lost your bait, never reel the line all the way in so the hook gets jammed in the rod. Always look behind you when you cast, so a hook doesn't snag someone in the head. And be careful on the boat when you're moving around so you don't fall into the water."

Within thirty minutes, my older son was flopping the fish into the boat, swinging the hook backward without looking, and reeling in the hook for more bait all the way to the tip of the rod. My younger son ran around the boat to cast willy-nilly in every direction. My wife and I kept reminding them of the rules, but they had turned stone-deaf.

At our last fishing spot, where the bay meets the Gulf, the action was nonstop, with Will and Scott catching ladyfish and sea trout and Captain Tom shouting at both of them.

"Wait, Will, what did I tell you, don't reel the hook all the way into the rod!"

"No, Scott, don't pull the fish all the way into the boat, let me get it!"

"Hey, both of you kids, I just said not to do that!"

"What did I just tell you guys!"

"Hang on, you nearly hooked your dad in the eye!"

"No, no, let me bait the shrimp!"

Captain Tom sprinted away from the wheel and grabbed the rod from Will, yelling, "Wait a second, wait a second, you're not doing that right!" Then he whipped around to tell Scott, "Didn't I just tell you not to do that!"

The two would heed one direction while forgetting the others. Will seemed to be willfully ignoring Captain Tom as he competed with his younger brother to land the biggest fish of the day.

At one brief break in the action, Captain Tom turned to look at us and said, "So, I guess you two must drink a lot."

32

MG

Hello, Delicious

"I hope you're drinking again—,
Life's too short."

—LETTER FROM HARRY

Could this letter have come at a better time with its almost unassailable argument? Just when we'd finished writing this book?

The irony had me laughing so hard I almost measured out a couple of fingers of the Absolut and a splash of vermouth from the bottles I considered hauling out to the dumpster together with the Gordon's gin and Jack Daniels. They've been hanging out in my cupboard for a long time. Why don't I toss them out?

"Yes, why don't you?" asks one of my fellow addicts in the circle at the clinic. "It's dangerous keeping booze so close at hand."

I answer with a shrug. "I know I'm not going to drink them."

"Then why do you keep them?"

Does she really think that's a sly response?

I don't answer. I don't know.

That was a long time ago, and I still don't know. I still have the bottles waiting for the Dumpster.

After all the arguments that tell you to stop drinking, there's only one telling you to keep on: that you can't stand not having that fiery slug of vodka or whiskey going down your throat and wearing down the rough edges of the day.

That's not an argument, is it? That's a statement of desire, a need. Yet that need is the first hurdle and the last hurdle that an alcoholic has to jump. When all the arguments have been put forth, what it comes down to is that you don't want to stop, because you'd lose that drink.

It's that one drink. The trouble is, you think of that one drink. It's always one. It's thinking about the drink that fires up your imagination, and imagination here is a killer.

(What you should do, as I have said elsewhere, and what the secret is—if there is one, and I think this is it—is follow that one drink to the second, the third, the fourth, the fifth, to the slip on the front steps, the hangover, the remorse.)

If that's the secret, why is it parenthetical? Because you don't give a damn when that one drink is sitting on the bar before you or delivered on a silver tray, you don't care at all about the trip to Remorse.

Recently, I read a description of that one drink written by an alcoholic who hadn't had a drink in a decade. He was in a bar for some more somber reason than drinking, and the bartender mistakenly placed a drink before him . . . well. His description of the drink just sitting there was enough to make an alcoholic weep. It was almost to his mouth before he set it back on the bar.

Here is an ad for a new vodka, and it's the most seductive advertisement I have ever seen: a woman's shoulders in wine-colored velvet; hair the color of brandy falling over her eyes so that we see only the lowered lid and lashes of one; claret-red lips just a breath away from the rim of a martini glass, the vodka looking like liquid silver. Her lips hover over the glass. The caption reads: "Hello, Delicious."

Not only the words themselves but the sound of them—that gentle sibilance. The look of the stemmed glass, the whispery sound of the words. Combine this with Forster's "Only connect," and that would be my answer to "Why do you drink?"

I return to the drawing room of the London hotel in Chelsea, the dark wood paneling, the deep cushions and wing chairs, the fire, the flowers in huge vases, the white-jacketed porter bearing a martini on a silver tray.

Hello, Delicious.

"If it's all of those details that attract you," says the good doctor who runs the clinic, "why not just fill the glass with water?" Because it's all illusion (they would have said in the clinic); all of those details are a kind of drinking bribery. It's as illusory as your old friend Gordon.

Why not sit with your buddies in Swill's and just, well, drink water instead of vodka? Why? Because the fireplace, the porter, the silver tray are all part of that drink.

I listened to an interview with the late Christopher Hitchens, who at the time was in the last stages of esophageal cancer. He said he had no doubt that the cancer was caused by his excessive smoking and drinking. He'd known the dangers of both; he'd taken the gamble, he said, and lost. But he could not imagine never drinking wine again, sitting around the table at a dinner party, the wine enriching conversation, or not having the edge that drinking and smoking put on his writing.

I wonder how Christopher Hitchens would have reacted had the interviewer said, "But that's all illusion, isn't it? All of the claptrap about enriched conversation, about a writing edge—isn't that sort of embroidery a form of denial?"

Christopher Hitchens probably would have looked thoughtful (to be polite) and then said something like "No. It's the truth. It's a drug. There's a rush. Don't you get it?"

"My old friend Jim Beam." This is a standing joke among alcoholics. It's famous. Only it isn't a joke when you come down to it. Taking the last of the empties out to the trash really does feel like throwing away a friend. And I think any alcoholic will tell you, there's simply no friend like that old friend, the first drink of the evening.

I remember a movie in which the daughter of wealthy parents had come for dinner. There was no alcohol served because the father was a recovering alcoholic. Afterward, the girl and her mother were talking about the father, and the mother said ruefully that she had liked him better when he was drinking. That was a shocking admission, she knew, about herself. But he had lost a spark, something that made their lives more enjoyable. Since he'd stopped drinking, he was sad a lot of the time.

In my clinic, I think they would come down hard on this

woman; they'd call her an enabler. But she wasn't: She had never done anything to undermine her husband's earnest effort to stay sober. I thought she was being devastatingly honest.

Where am I in my life except toward the end of it, standing at a Dumpster with a fifth of Absolut and a bottle of vermouth. If I were to take them inside and pour them in a shaker, what then? As Harry says, life is too short. There isn't enough time left to do much damage. I think of that seductive ad, the woman with her lips so near the glass. "Only connect," said E. M. Forster. This was the connection, not simply with other people but with myself and with the world.

I tip this ancient bottle of Absolut into the Dumpster and hope it doesn't smash. I hope it lands on some sort of soft bed of eggshells and ashes.

I don't hear a thing.

Goodbye, Delicious.